Richmond County, Virginia

Order Book Abstracts
1704-1705

Ruth and Sam Sparacio

The Antient Press Collection
from

Colonial Roots
Millsboro, Delaware
2016

Colonial Roots

Helping You Grow Your Family Tree

ISBN 978-1-68034-321-2

RICHMOND COUNTY, VIRGINIA
ORDER BOOK NO. 4
1704-1708

p.
1

At a Court held for Richmond County the first day of November 1704

Present

Lieut. Coll. GEORGE TAYLOR   Capt. JOHN DEANE

Capt. WILLIAM UNDERWOOD   Capt. JOHN TARPLEY   Justices

- This day the Letter of Attorney made by HENRY ROBINSON to WILLIAM WOODBRIDGE was proved by the Oath of DOMINICK BENNEHAN, one of the witnesses thereto, and ordered to be recorded

- This day THOMAS PEARCE confest Judgment to HENRY ROBINSON for seventeen pounds of sweet sented tobbo. in caske convenient to water in Northfarnham which is ordered to be paid with costs of suite als exo.

- Ordered by this Court that Mr. DANIEL McCARTY and Mr. GEORGE (blurred) entered Attorneys for our Sovereigne Lady the Queen dureing the (blurred)

- Upon the information of the Grand Jury of this County against MARY (blurred) for having a bastard Child, who be summoned to appeare att this Court to answer the said presentment, and failing therein, Judgment is therefore granted to the Churchwardens of Sittenbourne Parish for the use of the said Parish. JOHN RICHENSEN, Security, returned for her appearance for five hundred pounds of tobbo. which is ordered to be paid als exo.

- The presentment of the Grand Jury against AVERY NAYLER for hanging tobbo. on the Sabbath Day is continued till next Court

- Ordered that DANLL. McQUIRE and ANNE JEFFEREYS be summoned to appeare at the next Court to give theire evidence against the said AVERY NAYLER in the presentment of the Grand Jury against him

- The presentment of the Grand Jury against RICHARD HILL, Ordinary Keeper, for selling drink on the Sabbath Day is dismist

- The presentment of the Grand Jury against EDWARD JEFFEREYS for selling drink on the Sabbath Day is dismist.

p.
2.

Richmond County Court 1st of November 1704.

- The presentment of the Grand Jury of this County against SHILAH, the Wife of EDWARD NEWTON for speaking Blasphemy is dismist

- Upon the presentment of the Grand Jury of this County against JOHN CARY and KATHERINE OBLIN for goeing to bed together as man and wife, the Court have odered that if the said KATHERINE OBLIN do not appeare att the next Court to answer the said presentment, that she be mulcted according to the Court's direction for her contempt.

- Upon the Petition of DANIELL McCARTY, Order for administration is granted to him on all and singular the Estate of DARBY ENGLISHBY, he giving security according to Law

- This day, WILLIAM WOODBRIDGE and DANIELL McCARTY acknowledged themselves indebted unto the worspll. her Majties. Justices for Richmond County in the full and just sum of Ten thousand pounds of tobbo. to be paid to the said

Justices theire Exrs. and Admrs. in case the said DANLL. McCARTY do not duely administer on all and singular the Estate of DARBY ENGLISHBY, deced., and render a true account thereof when he shall be thereunto lawfully called als exo.

- Ordered that Mr. SAMLL. BAYLY, Mr. RICHARD GREENE, Mr. GEORGE HEALE and Mr. DAVID BERWICK or any three of them do meet att the house of DARBY ENGLISHBY, deced., sometime betweene this and the next Court and do then and there inventory and appraise all and singular the Estate of the said deced., as the same shall come to theire view and make Report of theire proceedings therein to the said next Court under their hands in writing. Capt. THOMAS BEALE is requested to administer an Oath to the Appraisers for the true appraismt. of the said deced.'s Estate as also to the Administrator for the true discovery thereof

- The Petition of DANIELL McCARTY for the tutoridge of SAMLL. ENGLISHBY, Son of DARBY ENGLISHBY, is refferred till next Court

- Upon the Petition of JOSEPH RUSSELL, ordered that the ear marke of his hoggs & cattle be recorded

- This day the Inventory of Appraisment of the Estate of NICHOLAS LEWIS being presented to this Court by CHARLES SPOO, the same is ordered to be recorded

- Ordered that the Account of CHARLES SPOO against the Estate of NICHOLAS LEWIS be recorded

- This day the valuation and appraisment of an acre of land for DANLL. McCARTY to build a Mill upon, being by him presented to this Court,

p.   Richmond County Court 1st of November 1704
3   ordered that the same be recorded and that he pay the sume of twenty shillings according to the said valuation to such person or persons unto whome the said Land shall of right belong or lawfull appertaine

- This day the valuation and appraisment of an acre of land for Mr. GEORGE GLASCOCK to build a Mill upon being presented into Court by Mr. DANLL. McCARTY, the same is ordered to be recorded; And it is ordered that the said GEORGE do pay the summe of two hundred pounds of tobbo. according to the returne of the said valuation to such person or persons unto whome the said land shall of right belong or lawfully appertaine

- This day the Letter of Attorney made by Mr. THOMAS CRESSEY to JOHN HARPER was proved by the Oathes of DAVID CROSSE and DOMINICK BENNEHAN, witnesses thereto, and ordered to be recorded

- This day WILLIAM STEPHENSON came into Court and by and with his owne consent acknowledged that he was willing to serve Mr. JOHN HARPER the full trme of six yeares according to an Instrument in Writing under the hands and seals of the said WILLIAM and JOHN, wch: is ordered to be recorded

- Upon the Petition of EDWARD TURBERVILL and ANNE his Wife, Father and Mother in Law to WILLIAM and RALPH SIZE, Sons of JOHN SIZE, deced., ordered that the said WILLIAM and RALPH do continue with and serve the said EDWARD and ANNE his Wife till they shall attaine to the age of twenty one yeares, the said EDWARD oblidging himselfe to learne them to read, write and cypher and it is ordered that the said EDWARD enter into Bond wth: sufficient security for five thousand pounds of tobbo. to accomplish and performe the same

- This day, MARGT. LAMB, came into Court and acknowledged that JOHN REYNOLDS was Father to a bastard Child borne of her body

- This day, MARGT. LAMB by and with her owne consent, came into Court and obliged her selfe to serve her present Master, WILLIAM PANNELL the full terme of one whole yeare after her time by Indenture Custome or otherwise be fully expired in satisfaction of his paying her Fine for committing the sin of fornication and having a bastard Child

- Ordered that MARGT. LAMB, Servant to WILLIAM PANNELL, do serve her said Master or his assignes according to Law in compensation for the trouble of his House during the time of her Child birth

- This day, WILLIAM PANNELL confest Judgment to the Church Wardens of Sittenbourne Parish for the use of the Parish for five hundred pounds of tobbo., it being the Fine of MARGT. LAMB for committing the sin of fornication &

p. <u>Richmond County Court 1st of November 1704</u>
4   having a bastard Child and it is ordered that he pay the same als exo.

- This day, NEBUCHADENEZER JONES confessed Judgment to the Church Wardens of Sittenbourne Parish for the use of the said Parish for five hundred pounds of tobbo, it being the Fine of MARY BRADGATE for committing the sin of fornication and having a bastard Child and it is ordered that he pay the same als exo.

- Ordered that MARY BRADGATE by and with her owne consent, do serve her present Master, NEBUCHADENEZER JONES the full terme of one whole yeare being in satisfaction for his paying of her Fine for committing the sin of fornication and having a bastard Child

- Ordered that JOHN REYNOLDS be summoned to appeare att the next Court held for this County and that he do then and there enter into bond with sufficient security to indemnify and keep harmless the Church Wardens of Sittenbourne Parish for and by reason of bastard Child layd to him and borne of the body of MARGT. LAMB

- It evidently appearing to this Court that MARY BRADGATE had fugitively absented her selfe from the service of her Master, NEBUCHADENEZER JONES the space of sixty nine days and that he had expended the summe of one hundred pounds of tobbo. to procure her againe. Ordered that the said MARY BRADGATE do serve the said NEBUCHADENEZER JONES or his assignes ye said terme of sixty nine days after her time by Indenture contracted for be expired and that she pay to the said NEBUCHADENEZER JONES the sume of one hundred pounds of tobbacco att the time aforesaid

- This day LAWRENCE CALLAHAN by and with his owne consent oblidged him selfe to serve WILLIAM SMOOT the terme of nine months after his time by Indenture be expired upon condition that the said WILLIAM do teach him to write read & cypher within the time aforesaid

- This day MARY NORTHCUTT came into Court and bound her Son, RICHARD WHITE to JOHN CANTERBURY till he should attaine to the age of twenty one yeares, he being twelve yeares old the seventeenth day of February next

- Ordered that WILLIAM MORGAN do serve his Unkle, WILLIAM YATES, untill he shall arrive to the age of twenty one yeares, the said WILLIAM YATES oblidging him selfe to teach him the Trade of a Carpenter to the best of his knowledge within the said terme, upon this condition, nevertheless, that if the said WILLIAM

MORGAN can make sufficient proofe that it was the

p.   <u>Richmond County Court 1st of November 1704</u>
5   Will of his Mother that he should be free att the age of eighteene yeares that then in such case the said WILLIAM MORGAN be free att the age of eigh-teene yeares as aforesaid

- This day STANLEY GOWER acknowledged a Deed for Land to DAVID BER-WICK wch: is ordered to be recorded

- This day DAVID BERWICK acknowledged a Deed for Land to STANLEY GOVER which is ordered to be recorded

- This day STANLEY GOWER acknowledged an Assignment of a Deed for Land made by DAVID BERWICK to him to WILLIAM CLAYTON, which is ordered to be recorded

- This day SAMUELL SAMFORD acknowledge a Deed for Land to DANLL. McCARTY wch: is ordered to be recoded

- Pursuant to an Order of Court the 3d day of August 1704, granted upon the Petition of MARY GILBERT for the (C   ) of JOHN MILLS, Exectr. of the Last Will & Testament of JAMES GILBERT, deced., to prove the Will of the said JAMES ac-coring to due form of Law, it only being proved in (   ) form, the said MILLS accor-dingly appeared & MARY GILBERT by her Atto:, GEO: ESKRIDGE, not insisting on any further proofe by ye sd. Will than already made but did by his pleading make voyd the same & all dependence and evidences in order to prove the sd. JAMES in his life time revoaked the said Will. The Court on ye consideration of ye whole matter are of Judgment that the Will of the said JAMES GILBERT is a good Will and duely proved & that the evidences produced to prove the revocation thereof are not sufficient in the Law to prove the said revocation, from wch: Judgment (upon reading the Order) the said MARY GILBERT by her Attorney, GEORGE ESKRIDGE, did appeale to the 5th day of the next Generall Court and upon the motion of the said MARY GILBERT by her aforesaid Atto:, GEORGE ESKRIDGE (the Evidences produced to prove the abovesd. revocation being put into writing & severally sworne to in Court) are ordered to be recorded

From which Judgment the said MARY GILBERT by her Attorney GEORGE ESKRIDGE appeales to the 5th day of the next Generall Court

- This day SAMUELL SAMFORD and EDWARD JONES acknowledged them selves indebted to the Worsppll. her Majties. Justices of Richmond County in the full and just summe of twenty thousand pounds of good tobbo. and caske to be paid to the said Justices their Exrs. and Admrs. in case MARY GILBERT do not prosecute an appeale by her made from an Order of this Court this day obtained against her by JOHN MILLS, Exr. of JAMES GILBERT, to the 5th day of the next Generall Court

- The Court adjourned till tomorrow eight p Clock

p.   <u>Att a Court held for Richmond County ye Second day of November 1704</u>
6   Present her Majties Justices
Lieut. Coll. GEORGE TAYLOR   Capt. JNO: DEANE
Lieut. Coll. SAMLL. PEACHEY   Capt. JNO: TARPLEY

- This day Majr. WILLIAM ROBINSON and FRANCES his Wife acknow-ledged a Deed for Land to Mr. JAMES SHERLOCK, and the said FRANCES ROBIN-

SON being duely examined according to Law, said that shee voluntarily and with her owne consent without any manner of compulsion acknowledged the said Deed, and it is ordered that the same be recorded

- This day WILLIAM WOODBRIDGE came into Court and entered GEORGE ESKRIDGE his Attorney for one whole yeare

- The action brought by JOHN CHAMP against THOMAS LEWIS is dismist, Plt. not prosecuting

- Especiall imparlance is granted in the suite betweene JAMES PHILLIPS, Plt. and HONOR WOFFENDALL, Exrx, Defendt. till next Court

- Especiall imparlance is granted in the suite of HONOR WOFFENDALL, Exrx. of ADAM WOFFENDALL, deced., Plt. and JAMES PHILLIPS, Deft. till next Court

- Especiall imparlance is granted in the suite betweene SAMLL. BAYLY, Plt. and GEORGE BRUCE, Defendt., till next Court

- The action brought by HENRY HAWS vs. JOHN HAWKSFORD is dismist, the Plt. not prosecuting

- The action brought by ROBERT MOSELEY vs. JOHN BIRKETT is continued till next Court

- The action brought by JOHN WORDEN against JOHN JONES, Shoemaker, is continued till next Court

- Especiall imparlance is granted in the suite betweene JOHN WORDEN, Plt. and FRANCIS WILLIAMS, Defendt, till next Court

- This day JOHN JONES, Shoemaker, confest Judgment to JOHN WORDEN for twelve hundred and ninety pounds of tobbo. and caske convenient to water in Richmond County, which is ordered to be paid with costs of suite als exo.

p.   Richmond County Court 2nd of November 1704
7   - In the action of Case betweene JOHN WORDEN, Plt. and RICHARD
        WISDELL, Defendt., for eight hundred and thirty two pounds of tobbo. by account, the said Defendt. being called & not appearing nor any security returned, Judgment is therefore granted to the Plt. against the Sheriff for the said summe of eight hunded and thirty two pounds of tobbo. unless the said Defendt. appeare att the next Court and answer the said action

- Judgment being this day past against the Sheriff for eight hundred and thirty two pounds of tobbo. unto JOHN WORDEN for the non appearance of RICHARD WISDELL att the suite of the said JOHN, upon the motion of the Sheriff, Attachment is granted to him against the Estate of the said RICHARD WISDELL for the said sume of eight hundred and thirty two pounds of tobbo. returnable to the next Court for Judgment

- In the action of Debt betweene JOHN WORDEN, Plt. and KATHERINE HENDERKIN, Deft., for seven hundred and twenty four pounds of tobbo. and caske convenient to water in Richmond County, the said Defendt. being called and not appearing nor any security returned, Judgment is therefore granted to the Plt. for the summe aforesd. unless the said Defendt. appeare att the next Court and answer the said action

- Nonsuite is granted to JOHN LANE for the non appearance of HENRY TODD, wch. is ordered to be paid wth: costs of suite als exo.

- The action brought by JOHN LANE against HENRY TODD is dismist, the

Plt. not prosecuting.

- The action brought by THOMAS GLADMAN against THOMAS LOYD, Taylor, is dismist, the Plt. not prosecuting

- In an action of Debt between SAMLL. BAYLY, Plt. and EDWARD YOUNG, Defendt., for two hundred and seven pounds of tobbo., and the said Defendt. being called and not appearing, Judgmt. is therefore granted to the Plt. against WILLIAM LAMBERT, Security returned for his apperance for the sume aforesaid unless the Defendt. appears att the next Court and answers the said action

- The action brought by JAMES INGO against SAMUELL (   ) is dismist, the Plt. not prosecuting

- In an action of Case betweene JAMES INGO, Plt. and JAMES PHILLIPS, Defendt., for two hundred and twenty five pounds of tobbo., the said Defendt. being called and not appearing nor any security returned, Judgment is therefore granted to the Plt. against the Sheriff for the said summe of two hundred twenty five pounds of tobbo. unless the said Defendt. appeare att the next Court and answer the said action

p.   Richmond County Court 2nd of November 1704
8   - Judgment being this day past against the Sheriff for two hundred and twen-
        ty five pounds of tobbo. to JAMES INGO for the non appearance of JAMES
PHILLIPS att the suite of the said JAMES INGO, upon motion of the Sheriff Attachment is granted unto him against the Estate of the said JAMES PHILLIPS for the summe of tobbo. aforesaid returnable to the next Court for Judgmt.

- In an action of Debt betweene THOMAS WHITE, Plt. and THOMAS DEAKUS, Defendt., for five hundred and nineteene pounds of tobbo. convenient to water in Richmond County, the Sheriff having returned the Defendt. by a coppy left. Atta. is therefore granted the Plt. against the Estae of the said Defendt. for the abovesd. summe of tobbo. returnable to the next Court for Judgmt.

- In an action of Debt betweene THOMAS WHITE, Plt. and WILLIAM SMITH, Cordwainer, Defendt. for four hundred and ninety foure pounds of tobbo., in caske, the said Defendt. being called and not appeareing nor any security returned, Judgment is therefore granted to the Plt. against the Sheriff. for the aforesaid summe unless the said Defendt. appeare att the next Court and answer the said action

- Judgment being this day past against the Sheriff for foure hundred and ninety foure pounds of tobbo. in caske unto THOMAS WHITE for the non appeare-ance of WILLIAM SMITH, Shoemaker, att the suite of the said THOMAS, upon the motion of the Sheriff, Attachment is granted him against the Estate of the said WIL-LIAM SMITH for the said summe of tobbo. returnable to the next Court for Judgmt.

- The action brought by THOMAS WHITE against ROBERT PAINE is con-tinued till next Court

- In an action of Debt betweene THOMAS WHITE, Plt. and GARRARD NEWTON, Defendt. for three hundred and twenty pounds of tobbo. of his own planta-tion growth due by Bill, and the Sheriff haveing returned the Defendt. by a Coppy left, Attachment is therefore granted to the Plt. against the Estate of the said Defendt. for the said summe of tobbo. returnable to the next Court for Judgment

- This day SAMLL. SAMFORD, Executor of the Last Will and Testament of JAMES SAMFORD of the Parish of Northfarnham & County of Richmond, deced., confest Judgmt. to ALEXANDER (   ) of Christ Church Parish and County of

LANCASTER for two thousand eight hundred and five pounds of good sound tobbo. and caske att the Plantation of the said deced., on RICHARDSONS CREEKE wch. this

p.   Richmond County Court 2nd of November 1704
9.   Court have ordered to be paid with costs of suit als exo.
- This day the Last Will and Testament of JAMES SAMFORD being presented to the Court by the Executor therein named for proofe, the same was proved by the Oath of EDWARD JONES, and it is ordered that the Probate thereof be continued till next Court for the appeareance of GYLES WEBB & RICHARD TAYLER the other evidences to the said Will.
- The action brought by THOMAS WHITE against HONOR WOFFENDALL is continued till next Court
- This day JOHN JONES, Shoemaker, confest Judgment to NICHOLAS SMITH for two thousand three hundred and one pounds of tobbo. this this Court have ordered to be payd wth: costs of suite als exo.
- In an action of Debt betweene WILLIAM STONE, Assignee of JAMES PHILLIPS, JR., Plt. and WILLIAM BOWLIN, Deft., for one thousand and fifty pounds of tobbo. due by Bill to be paid convenient to water in Richmond County and the Defendt being by the Sheriff returned by a Copy left, Attachment is therefore granted to the Plt. against the Estate of the said Defendt. for the said summe of tobbo. returnable to the next Court for Judgmt.
- The action brought by MARKE (? AYNOR) against WM. BOWLIN is dismist the Plt. not prosecuting
- In an action of Debt between ANTHONY SEALE, Plt. and ROBT. LEGG, Defendt., for six hundred and seventy eight pounds of tobbo. in caske convenient to water in Richmond County and the Sheriff haveing returned the Defendt. by a copy left and failing to appeare, Attachment is therefore granted to the Plt. against the Estate of the said Defendt. for the summe aforesaid returnable to the next Court for Judgment
- The action brought by JAMES NELSON and ELIZABETH his Wife against WILLIAM SEARLES is dismist, the Plts. not prosecuting
- The action brought by THOMAS NEWMAN against WILLIAM SEARLES is dismist, the Plt. not prosecuting
- Nonsuite is granted to JOHN CHAMP for the non appeareance of RICHARD WOOD which is ordered to be paid wth: costs als exo.
- The action brought by JAMES GRAHAM against EDWARD NEWTON is continued till next Court

p.   Richmond County Court 2nd of November 1704
10   - Nonsuite is granted to JOHN CHAMP for the non appeareance of JOHN LOYD, Esqr., wch. is ordered to be paid wth: costs als exo.
- The action brought by GARRARD LYNCH againt RICHARD FOX is continued till next Court
- The action brought by SAMLL. SAMFORD against Collo. GEORGE MASON of STAFFORD County is dismist, the Plt. not prosecuting
- The Ejectione firma brought by JAMES TARPLEY against WILLIAM

BARBER is continued till next Court

  - The action brought by THOMAS WHITE against JOHN DALTON is continued till next Court

  - The Scire Facias brought by ANDREW CROMWELL and Capt. ROBERT McCARREL of the Kingdome of Ireland against JOHN DALTON and MARY his Wife, Admrx. of the Estate of WILLIAM BROCKENBROUGH, deced., is continued till next Court

  - The action brought by GEORGE MASON and HUGH HAYWARD against CHARLES DODSON is dismist, the Plts. not prosecuting

  - The action brought by THOMAS MACKEY vs. JOHN DALTON is continued till next Court

  - The action brought by THOMAS MACKEY against JOHN WHITE is dismist the Plt. not prosecuting

  - The action brought by THOMAS MACKEY against THOMAS WHITE is continued till next Court

  - The action brought by JAMES PHILLIPS against JOHN DALTON is dismist, the Plt. not prosecuting

  - The action brought by DAVID BERWICK, Atto. of JOSHUA WHITING, against JOHN CHILSON is dismist, the Plt. not prosecuting

  - The action brought by JAMES INGO against JOHN DALTON is continued till next Court

  - The action brought by SAMLL. SAMFORD against GEORGE BEWFORD is dismist, the Plt. not prosecuting

  - The action brought by SEM COX agaisnt JOHN DALTON is continued till next Court

p.   Richmond County Court 2nd of November 1704)
11   - The action brought by JAMES CAWARD against WILLIAM NORRIS is dismist, the Plt. not prosecuting

  - Judgment being this day past against the Sheriff for seven hundred and twenty foure pounds of tobbo. and caske convenient to water in Richmond County unto JOHN WORDEN for the non appeearence of KATHERINE HENDERKIN at the suite of the said JOHN, upon the motion of the Sheriff Attachment is granted him against the Estate of the said KATHERINE HENDERKIN for the aforesaid summe of tobbo. returnable to the next Court for Judgmt.

  - The Court is adjourned till the first Wednesday in December next

  - Att a Court held for Richmond County the 6th day of December 1704
                        Present
Lieut. Coll. GEORGE TAYLER   Capt. JOHN DEANE
Lieut. Coll. SAMLL. PEACHEY   Capt. JOHN TARPLEY   Justices
Capt. WILLIAM UNDERWOOD

  - The action brought by JOHN LOYD, Esqr., who as well for and on behalfe of our Sovereigne Lady the Queene as for and on behalfe of himselfe against JOHN CHAMP is dismist, ye Plt.'s Attorney being dead

  - The action brought by JOHN HIGGINS against GARRARD LYNCH is dismist, the Plt. not prosecuting

    - In an action of Case betweene JOSHUA HIGHTOWER, Plt. and JOB HAMMOND, Defendt., for six hundred pounds of tobbo. upon a Bond, and the said Defendt. being called and not appeareing nor any security returned, Judgment is therefore granted to the Plt. against the Sheriff for the said summe of six hundred pounds of tobbo. unless the said Defendt. appeare att the next Court and answers the said action

    - Judgment being this day past against the Sheriff for six hundred pounds of tobbo. to JOSHUA HIGHTOWER for the non appeareance of JOB HAMMOND att the suite of the said JOSHUA, upon the motion of the Sheriff, Atta. is granted unto him against the Estate of the said JOB for the summe of six hundred pounds of tobbo. returnable to the next Court for Judgmt.

p.   Richmond County Court 6th of December 1704)
12   - The action brought by HENRY PARRY agt. DAVID GWYN is dismist, the Defendt. being dead

    - The action brought by HENRY ROBINSON against Mr. THOMAS CRESSEY is dismist, the Plt. not prosecuting

    - This day the Last Will and Testament of JOHN SUGGETT being presented to this Court for proofe, the same was proved by the Oath of JAMES MURPHEY and the Probate thereof continued for the other wittnesses to give evidence to the proofe of the said Will

    - Upon the Petition of THOMAS DICKENSON, ordered that the Eare marke of his hoggs and cattle, being a crop & two slitts and an under keele on the right eare and a crop & two slitts and an under keele on the left eare be recorded

    - The proofe of the Last Will and Testament of JAMES SAMFORD continued till next Court for another evidence

    - This day the Inventory and Appraisment of the Estate of WILLIAM GLOW being presented to this Court by EDWARD JONES, the same is ordered to be recorded

    - JOHN GLOW in open Court this day made choice of SYMON TAYLER for his Guardian and it is ordered that the said SYMON TAYLER do take into his custody the Estate of the said JOHN GLOW wch. was left to him by his Unkle and Godfather of the said JOHN

    - This day RICHARD FOX confest Judgment to GARRARD LYNCH for three hundred pounds of tobbo. upon balla. of a Bill wch: is ordered to be aid with costs of suite als exo.

    - This day NATHANLL. POPE, Atto. for and on behalfe of MARY TRIPLETT, Admrx. of FANCIS TRIPLETT, confest Judgment to ABIGAILE TRIPLETT for one thousand one hundred and thirty six pounds of tobbo. wch: this Court have ordered to be paid wth: costs of suite als exo.

    - Upon Petition of Capt. CHARLES BARBER, Sheriff of this County, concerning the summoning of a Jury and his attendance upon a Survey in the suite betweene JOHN LOYD, Esqr., Plt. and JOHN CHAMP, Defendt., ordered that

p.   Richmond County Court 6th of December 1704
13   he be paid by the said JOHN LOYD the summe of five hundred pounds of

tobbo. for his trouble therein als exo.

    - This day JOHN REYNOLDS acknowledged a Deed of Land wth: Bond to Coll. RICHARD TALIAFERRO which is ordered to be recorded

    - Mr. JOSHUA DAVIS by virtue of a Warrant of Attorney from the said RICHARD TALIAFERRO to him directed, reserved the acknowledgment of the said Deed wch: is ordered to be recorded

    - This day JAMES INNIS acknowledged a Deed for Land to ROBERT CARTER, Esqr., which is ordered to be recorded

    - This day JAMES INNIS acknowledged a Deed for Land to ROBERT CARTER, Esqr., which is ordered to be recorded

    - This day JAMES INNIS acknowledged a Deed for Land to ROBERT CARTER, Esqr. which is ordered to be recorded

    - This day JAMES STORY, Atto. for and on the behalfe of KATHERINE INNIS, Wife of JAMES INNIS, relinquished her Right of Dower to three several Deeds for Land by the said JAMES INNIS this day acknowledged to ROBERT CARTER, Esqr., which is ordered to be recorded

    - Upon the Petition of Madam KATHERINE GWYN, Widdo. & Relict of Majr. DAVID GWYN, late of this County, deced., thereby setting forth that upon her intermarriage wth: Mr. WILLIAM FAUNTLEROY, her former Husband, deced., by one Indenture beareing date the 28th day of Febry. 1680, one messuage tenement and tract of land containing about twelve hundred acres butting and bounding as in the said Deed is mentioned and expressed, as also six Negroes in the said Deed particularly named, together with theire future increase and posterity, and all the goods and chattells and kitchen utensills particularly mentioned in a Schedule to the said Deed annexed, were conveyed by the said WILLIAM FAUNTLEROY and the said KATHERINE GWYN unto RICHARD LEE of WESTMORELAND County and LEROY GRIFFIN of RAPPA: County for the use of the said WILLIAM FAUNTLEROY dureing his naturall life and after his decease to the use of the said KATHERINE her heires, &c., as her Joynture in recompense of her Dower, and after the decease of the said WILLIAM and KATHERINE to the use of the heires of ye said WILLIAM and KATHERINE lawfully to be begotten. Your Petitioner humbly pryas ye Worspps. to appoint such persons as you shall think fitt to set aside to the said Petitioner what is thereby due and belonging unto her. Whereupon it is ordered that Coll. WILLIAM TAYLOE, Capt. JOHN TARPLEY, Capt. THOMAS BEALE and Mr. JAMES SHERLOCK, or any three of them, do meet att the house of the said Majr. DAVID GWYN on the eighteenth day of this instant December

p.   <u>Richmond County Court 6th of December 1704</u>
14   if faire if not on the next faire day after and do then and there lay out and
       separate the aforesaid Joynture so given and settled upon her as aforesaid from the Estate of the said Majr. DAVID GWYN according to the Schedule annexed and make Report of theire proceedings therein to the next Court under their hands in writing.

    - Pursuant to his Excellency's Directions, ordered that five pounds Sterl. put into the hands of Capt. CHARLES BARBER for the use of ANNE BAKER, Daughter in Law of JOHN BAKER, be disposed of as this Court shall think fitt for the purchasing of female cattle for the use of the said ANNE BAKER, the said CHARLES BARBER giveing security for the delivery of the said cattle for ye use aforesd.

- Certificate according to Act of Assembly is granted to THOMAS DICKEN-SON for one hundred and fifty acres of Land for the Importation of three people in this Colony by name MARGT. STEWARD, ELIZA: MORGAN & ANNE JEFFREYS, the said THOMAS makeing Oath that he nor any to his knowledge had received Certificate for the same

- Certificate according to Act of Assembly is granted to Capt. WILLIAM UNDERWOOD for two hundred acres of land for Importation of foure persons into this Colony by name, JOHN ASHBURY, ROBERT SMITH, ANTHO: FLANAGAN & MORGAN HOGAN, the said WM. UNDERWOOD makeing Oath that neither he nor any to his knowledge had received Certificate for the same, the Right of which he assigned in Court to THOMAS DICKENSON

- In the Ejectione firma brought by ---------- against ---------- the Sheriff makeing oath that he had served a coppy of the Declaration on ---------- tenant in possession, Ordered that unless the said ---------- appeare att the next Court Cause of Lease Entry and Ouster enter himselfe Defendt. in the said suite and onely upon the Tryall of the title, Judgment go against him by default. (the names in this suit were either deleted as in the first intance or written over making them illegible as in the other instances)

- This day JAMES SHERLOCK acknowledged a Deed of Lease and Release for Land wth: Bond to Capt. WM. ROBINSON, wch: is ordered to be recorded

- Certificate according to Act of Assembly is granted to GEORGE PAYNE for five hundred acres of land for Importation of ten persons into this Collony by name, HOWELL JONES, THOMAS PRENTICE, ELINOR SHARP, ANNE HARRISON, ELINOR SCOTT, PATRICK GIBBINS, DENNIS CONNOR, MARGARETT JAMES,

p.   Richmond County Court 6th of December 1704
15   CHARLES DAYLY & THOMAS HICKS, the said GEORGE PAYNE
        makeing Oath that neither he nor any to his knowledge had received Certificate for the same, the right of which he assigned in Court to Mr.EDWARD BARROW

- Certificate according to Act of Assembly is granted to JOHN ALLOWAY for two hundred acres of Land for Importation of foure persons into this Collony by name, JOHN ALLOWAY, MARGRETT WATTSEN, BETTY CROULTS, LEWIS THOMAS, the said JOHN makeing Oath that neither he nor any to his knowledge had received Certificate for the same, the right of wch: he assigned in Court to Mr. EDWARD BARROW

- Certificate according to Act of Assembly is granted to WILLIAM SMITH for three hundred and fifty acres of land for Importation of seven persons into this Collony by name, WILLIAM SMITH, ELIZA: JONES, ELIZA: JACKSON, HUMPHREY THOMAS, THOMAS JAMES, PETER (? CUMMADO) & THOMAS LUKE, the said WILLIAM SMITH makeing Oath tht neither he nor any to his knowledge had received Certificate for the same, the right of which he assigned in Court to Mr. EDWARD BARROW

- Certificate according to Act of Assembly is granted to JAMES CAWARD for one hundred and fifty acres of Land for Importation of three persons into this Collony by name, JAMES CAWARD, ROBERT (? ROWIN) & KATHERINE CLACK, the said JAMES makeing Oath that neither he nor any to his knowledge had received Certificate for the same, the Right of which he assigned in Court to Mr. EDWARD

BARROW.
    - Certificate according to Act of Assembly is granted to JAMES SUGGITT for one hundred and fifty acres of land for Importation of three persons into this Collony by name JOS: SHERDEN, JEANE TEBET and JAMES SMITH, the sd. SUGGITT makeing Oath tht neither he nor any to his knowledge had received Certificate for the same, the Right of which he assigned in Court to Mr. EDWARD BARROW

    - Certificte according to Act of Assembly is granted to JOSEPH DEEKE, for two hundred acres of land for Importation of foure persons into this Collony by name, JOSEPH DEEKE, JO: KEENE, JOS: HORE & ELIZA: DUGGAN, the said JOSEPH DEEKE makeing Oath that neither he nor any to his knowledge had received Certificate for the same, the Right of which he assigned in Court to Mr. EDWARD BARROW

p.   Richmond County Court 6th of December 1704
16   - Certificate according to Act of Assembly is granted to WILLIAM SMOOT
    for one hundred and fifty acres of land for Importation of three persons into this Collony by name PETER TEGLE, JO: MILLER & LAWRENCE CALLYHAN, the said WILLIAM makeing oath tht neither he nor any to his knowledge had received Certificate for the same, the Right of which he assigned in Court to Mr. EDWARD BARROW

    - Certificate according to Act of Assembly is granted to SAMLL. BAYLY for one hundred acres of land for Importation of two persons into this Collony by name THOMAS PORTWOOD & ROBERT HALL, the said SAMLL. makeing Oath that neither he nor any to his knowledge had received Certificate for the same, the Right of which he assigned in Court to Mr. EDWARD BARROW

    - This day the Inventory and Appraisment of the Estate of FRANCIS TRIP-LETT being presented to this Court by NATHANLL: POPE, the same is ordered to be recorded

    - Upon the motion of GARRARD LYNCH, ordered that he have tuition of SAMLL. INGLISHBY, Son of DARBY INGLISHBY, untill he shall arrive to the age of twenty one yeares and that the said GARRARD LYNCH do give Bond wth: sufficient security for ten thousand pounds of tobbo. to DANLL. McCARTY & FRANCIS LYNCH to learne the said SAMLL. to read write and cypher perfectly as farr as the Rule of Three, the said SAMLL. being att this time eight yeares of age

    - Upon the motion of DANLL. McCARTY, ordered that ANNE INGLISHBY do serve the said DANLL. McCARTY or his assignes the full terme of three yeares, the said DANLL. McCARTY obildging him selfe to do his utmost endeavour to learne the said ANNE INGLISHBY to read, sew, spin and knitt

    - Certificate according to Act of Assembly is granted to JOHN DALTON for three hundred acres of land for Importation of six persons into this Collony by name, ARTHUR McGUIRE, JO: BURD, ANNE SAMLL; JO: LYNEY, KATHERINE PARRY & ROBERT WILSON, the said JOHN DALTON makeing Oath that neither he nor any to his knowledge had received Certificate for the same, the Right of which he assigned in Court to Mr. EDWARD BARROW

    - Certificate according to Act of Assembly is granted unto JOHN WILLIAMS for

p.   Richmond County Court 6th of December 1704
17   two hundred and fifty acres of land for Importation of five persons into this
Collony by name JO: JOANES, JO: DAVIS, MARY GROFFY, HENRY
PERRY, HENRY OLLMS, the said JOHN WILLIAMS makeing Oath that neither
he nor any to his knowledge had received Certificate for the same, the Right of which
he assigned in Court to Mr. EDWARD BARROW

- Certificate according to Act of Assembly is granted to Mr. GEORGE GLAS-
COCK for one hundred and fifty acres of land for Importation of three persons into
this Collony by name, WALTER CUMMONS, ROBERT HOLMES & ELIZA. MOR-
RIS, the said GEORGE GLASCOCK makeing Oath that neither he nor any to his
knowledge had received Certificate for the same, the Right of which he assigned in
Court to Mr. EDWARD BARROW

- Certificate according to Act of Assembly is granted to JOHN HARRIS for
two hundred and fifty acres of land for importation of five persons into this Collony by
name, JOHN YOUNG, CHARLES COOPER, CHRISTOPHER HUSLEAD, JOHN
MAN & MARY COLDIN, the said JOHN HARRIS makeing Oath that neither he nor
any to his knowledge had received Certificate for the same, the Right of which he
assigned in Court to Mr. EDWARD BARROW

- The Citation brought by JOHN TARPLEY, JUNR., by his Guardian JOHN
TARPLEY against CHRISTOPHER ROBINSON & JUDITH his wife, THOMAS
GRIFFIN, Gentl., PETER PRESSLEY, Gentl. & WINIFRED his Wife, Exrx. of the
Last Will and Testament of CORBIN GRIFFIN, Gentl., date of MIDDLESEX County
deced., is continued till next Court att the request of the Defendts.

- This day the Grand Jury of this County haveing brought in theire presentments to this Court, It is thereupon ordered that the Sheriff of this County or his
Deputy do take into his Custody the severall persons by them presented and that he
take sufficient security for their appeareance att next Court to answer to the severall
presentments, and the said Grand Jury are dismist for this time and ordered to continue theire Enquiry and make presentments thereof to the next Aprill Court

- Ordered that WILLIAM CAMBELL be summoned by the Sheriff to the next
Court to answer the presentment of the Grand Jury for keeping company with MARY
RICHARDSON, haveing three Children, being generally suspected to live in adultery

- Ordered that ZACHARIAH NICHOLLS be summoned by the Sheriff to the
next Court to answer the presentment of the Grand Jury for keeping MARY
MALADY and haveing one bastard by her by his owne confession

p.   Richmond County Court 6th of December 1704
18   - Ordered that WILLIAM WOODBRIDGE be summoned by the Sheriff to the
next Court to answer the presentment of the Grand Jury for his keeping company wth: the Wife of ZACHARIAH NICHOLLS and being generally suspected to
live in adultery with her

- Ordered that ABRAHAM DAEL be summoned by the Sheriff to the next
Court to answer the presentment of the Grand Jury for goeing on the Sabbath Day
to look for Deer Skinns wch: was due to him

- Ordered that GILBERT CROSSWELL be summoned by the Sheriff to the
next Court to answer the presentment of the Grand Jury for his travelling on the
Sabbath Day

- Ordered that RICHARD WHITE be summoned by the Sheriff to the next Court to answer the presentment of the Grand Jury for his drinking and makeing merry at his House on the Sabbath Day with JOHN BROWNE and CORNELIUS HARKIN, and also for not goeing to Church for two moneths together

- Ordered that ALEXANDER CAMBELL be summoned by the Sheriff to the next Court to answer the presentment of the Grand Jury for carrying a Gunn up and downe the Roads on the Sabbath Day

- Ordered that RICHARD SMITH, PETER ALMORE

		THOMAS DURHAM
JOHN HANCOCK	GEORGE DEVENPORT	JOHN OLDHAM
PHILLIP HARRIS	JOHN TANTOR	THOMAS NEWTON
STEPHEN GUBTON	PETER ELLIS, JUNR.	JOSHUA STONE
CHARLES DODSON, JUNR.	THOMAS DODSON	SAMLL. JONES
JOHN ROBERTS	EDMOND OVERTON	THOMAS SHERLOCK
GILBERT CROSSWELL	WILLIAM WOOD	DENNIS CAMERON
WILLIAM CAMPBELL &	JOHN RANKIN	

be summoned by the Sheriff to the next Court to answer the presentment of the Grand Jury for theire not goeing to Church for two moneths together

- Ordered that CORNELIUS HARKIN be summoned by the Sheriff to the next Court to answer the presentment of the Grand Jury for his not goeing to Church on the Sabbath Day for two moneths together

- Ordered that THOMAS MARTON and JAMES PEARSON be summoned by the Sheriff to the next Court to answer the presentment of the Grand Jury for theire not goeing to Church for two moneths together

- Ordered that ANDREW HARRISON be summoned by the Sheriff to the next Court to answer the presentment of the Grand Jury for his Fishing on the Sabbath Day

- Ordered that WILLIAM HILL be summoned by the Sheriff to the next Court to answer the presentment of the Grand Jury for his Fishing on the Sabbath Day

p.   Richmond County Court 6th of December 1704
19   - Ordered that RICHARD GREENE be summoned by the Sheriff to the next Court to answer the presentment of the Grand Jury for his selling Rum and Sugar on the Sabbath Day

- Ordered that ABRAHAM HANNISON and MARTHA NEWDALL be summoned by the Sheriff to the next Court to answer the presentment of the Grand Jury for committing fornication

- Ordered that WILLIAM RICHARDSON be summoned by the Sheriff to the next Court to answer the presentment of the Grand Jury for hunting on the Sabbath Day.

- Ordered that ROGER RICHARDSON be summoned by the Sheriff to the next Court to answer the presentment of the Grand Jury for carrying a Gunn in the Woods on the Sabbath Day

- Ordered that NICHOLAS SMITH be summoned by the Sheriff to the next Court to answer the presentment of the Grand Jury for selling Rum on the Sabbath Day

- Ordered that WILLIAM GRANT, JOHN WARD, CHRISTOPHER EDRINGTON, RICHARD PAYNE, OWEN McCARTY and STEPHEN NOWLIN be summoned by the Sheriff to the next Court to answer the presentment of the Grand Jury for theire being Drunk on the Sabbath Day and CICELY JORDAN for

for suffering the aforesaid persons to drink sweare and sing att her House on the Sabbath Day

    - Ordered that THOMAS NEWMAN be summoned by the Sheriff to the next Court to answer the presentment of the Grand Jury for his being Drunk on ye Sabbath Day

    - Ordered that ELIZABETH JONES be summoned by the Sheriff to the next Court to answer the presentment of the Grand Jury for her haveing a bastard Child

    - Ordered that MARY CARTER be summoned by the Sheriff to the next Court to answer the presentment of the Grand Jury for her haveing a bastard Child

    - Ordered that the Surveyors of Highwayes in St. Mary's Parish be summoned to the next Court by the Sheriff to answer the presentment of the Grand Jury for theire not cleareing theire Highwayes

    - Ordered that ABRAHAM GOURD's Servant woman be summoned by the Sheriff to the next Court to answer the presentment of the Grand Jury for the burying of her bastard Child privately

    - In an Ejectione Firma depending in this Court betweene JAMES TARPLEY, Plt. & WILLIAM BARBER, Defendt., for ye Defendt. ousting the Plt. from a certaine tract of land situate lying and being in the Parish of Farnham & County aforesaid containing one hundred acres now in the possession of JNO: WILSON in this County, wch: JNO. TARPLEY, Gent., did devise the said JAMES TARPLEY for a terme of yeares not yet expired, Mr. THOMAS GRIFFIN haveing made Oath upon the Hold Evangelists of God that he had served JNO: WILSON Tenant in possession wth: a copy of the Plt.'s Declaration in this behalfe and the notice thereon endorsed. Ordered that unless the said JOHN WILSON, the Tenant in possession or those under whome he claymes haveing due notice of this Order by the Sheriff of this County do appeare att the next Court held for this County, confess Lease Entry & Ouster, enter him selfe Defendt. in ye name of ye sd. WILLIAM BARBER and insist only upon ye tryall of ye Title, Judgment to pass agt. him by default.

p.
20

Att a Court held for Richmond County the 7th day of December 1704
Present

Lieut. Coll. GEORGE TAYLER   Capt. JOHN TARPLEY

Lieut. Coll. SAMLL. PEACHEY   Mr. JOSHUA DAVIS   Justices

    - Ordered that the Lease made by JOHN CRASKE and ELIZABETH his Wife to WILLIAM WATTSEN be recorded

    - This day NICHOLAS CHRISTOPHER, Servant to PETER EVANS, came into Court and acknowledged that he was willing to serve his said Master or assignes till the last day of October next in consideration of the said PETER EVANS's acquitting the said NICHOLAS of all service that was due unto him for his running away and giving him a good suite of Kerby Cloathes, a Shirt, a paire of new shoes and stockins and hatt att the expiration of the said terme

    - Upon the Petition of JAMES INGO, JOHN INGO, WILLIAM SMOOT, ABRAHAM GOURD and RICHARD FOWLER, ordered that WILLIAM FITZHERBERT PETER ELMORE and ROBERT PALMER be summoned by the Sheriff of this County or his Deputy to meet upon the Land that formerly belonged to Mr. SAMLL. GRIFFIN lying neare the head of FARNHAM CREEKE betweene this and the next Court and do then and there give theire evidence to the best of theire knowledge where the first begining corner tree of the land formerly stood it now being downe and gone. Capt. JOHN TARPLEY is requested to administer an Oath to the persons aforesaid for their true delivery of the place abovesaid who are required to report the same to the said next Court under theire hands in writing

 - The Order for laying out and valueing an acre of ground for Capt. JOHN TARPLEY to build a Mill upon is continued till next Court

 - Judgment upon audit is granted to GEORGE PURVIS against THOMAS RICHARDSON for five hundred and forty eighty pounds of tobbo. which is ordered to be payd with costs of suite als exo.

 - Judgment upon Attachment is granted DAVID WILLIAMS against the Estate of THOMAS YATES for six hundred pounds of tobbo attached in the hands of the sd. Defendt. wch: is ordered to be paid wth: costs of suite als exo.

 - The action brought by NATHANLL. POPE als. BRIDGES of WESTMORE-LAND County agt. HENRY LONG is continued till next Court

 - The Ejectione firma brought by THOMAS FRESHWATER against WILLIAM SISSON is dismist, ye Plt. not prosecuting

p. Richmond County Court 7th of December 1704
21 - This day JAMES PHILLIPS confest Judgment to GAWIN CORBIN for
  seven hundred and ten pounds of tobbo. upon balla. of a Bill wch: is ordered to be payd wth: costs of suite als exo.

 - In the action of Case betweene RICHARD WASHBURNE, Plt. and JAMES TRENT, Defendt., for two hundred pounds of tobbo. damage by reason of the Defendt. taking up docking branding and detaineing from the Plt. one young Mare belonging unto him, the said Defendt. by his Atto., Capt. THOMAS GREGSON, came into Court and pleaded Not Guilty, whereupon the Jury was impannelled and sworne to try the matter in issue by name

GEORGE GLASCOCK	SAMLL. BAYLY	WILLIAM FITZHERBERT
RAWLEIGH DOWNEMAN	JAMES SUGGITT	JOHN SIMONS
JOHN DALTON	JOHN MILLS	ROBERT JORDAN
JOHN RANKIN	JNO; INGO &	JAMES INGO

who being returned brought in the following Verdict; We of the Jury do find for the Plt. five hundred pounds of tobbo. damage and his Mare to be returned, And upon the motion of GEORGE ESKRIDGE, Attorney for the Plt., the said Verdict is ordered to be recorded; And it is ordered that the sd. JAMES TRENT do pay the same to the Plt. and returne him his Mare together with costs of suite als exo.

 - Certificate according to Act of Assembly is granted to WILLIAM WOOD-BRIDGE for five hundred and fifty acres of land for importation of eleven persons into this Collony, by name;

JO. (? R---WALL)	RACHEL KNOWEL	JOHN MORGEN
JANE SALSBERRY	SARAY BERDOCK	JAMES SAMMON
JAMES COLEMAN	MARY GRIFFIN	ANN MARQUIS
MARGRETT FLOCIE	RICHARD SMITH	

the said WM. makeing Oath yt: neither he nor any to his knowledge had received Certificate for the same, the Rights of which he assigned in Court to Mr. EDWARD BARROW

 - Certificate according to Act of Assembly is granted to THOMAS BRADLEY for two hundred acres of Land for Importation of foure persons into this Collony by name, (the abstracter cannot read the last name of any of the three men and one woman), the sd. THOMAS BRADLEY makeing Oath that neither he nor any to his knowledge had received Certificate for the same, the Right of which he assigned in Court to Mr. EDWARD BARROW

    - Certificate according to Act of Assembly is granted to JOHN WILSON for two hundred and fifty acres of land for Importation of five persons into this Collony by name JAMES EARLE, ROBERT WILLIAMS, JAMES (? LAWE), JAMES ROYALL, and JOSEPH PRICE, the said JOHN WILSON makeing Oath that neither he nor any to his knowledge had received Certificate for the same, the Right of which he assigned in Court to Mr. EDWARD BARROW

    - The action brought by WILLIAM GORDEN against GEORGE BEWFORD is dismist, the Plt. not prosecuting

p.   Richmond County Court 7th of December 1704
22   - In the action of Trespass betweeen WINEFRED GLASCOCK by GEORGE GLASCOCK her prochein amy, Plt. and EVE SMITH, Defendt. for one hundred pounds Sterling damage by means of the Defendt. committing divers Trespass on a certaine parcel of land belonging to the Plt. scituate lying and being in the Parish of Northfarnham in the County aforesaid containeing One hundred and eighty acres or thereabouts as by the Plt.'s Declaration is sett forth, and an especiall Imparlance being granted in the said suite last October Court and the said Defendt. being called and failing to appeare att this Court, Judgment is therefore granted to the Plt. against the said Defendt. by default, and the Court not knowing the damage sustained by the Plt. in the premisses have ordered that the Sheriff of this County or his Deputy summon an able Jury of the most antient and able freeholders of the vicinage inhabitants as neare as may be to the land in controversie and now ways concerned neither by affinity consanguinity or interest to meet upon the land aforesaid together with Capt. CHARLES SMITH, Surveyor of this County, on the fifteenth day of this Instant December if faire if not the next faire day after and being first sworne before some one of her Majties. Justices of the Peace for this County, do survey and lay out the said land according to the most antient and reputed bounds of the Patent thereof, haveing regard to all other Elder Patents and evidences that shall be produced either by the Plt. or Defendt.and make report of theire proceedings therein together with the damages sustained by the Plt. by means of the Trespass aforesaid to the said next Court under theire hands in writing.

    - Especiall Imparlance is granted in the suite betweene CHRISTOPHER PRIDHAM Plt. and LEWIS RICHARDS of the Parish of Northfarnham and County of Richmond, Planter, Defendt., till next Court

    - Ordered that EDMOND McGLYNCHA be payd by RICHARD WASHBURNE for seven days attendance according to Act, being by him subpaened as an evidence in the suite betweene the said RICHARD, Plt. and JAMES TRENT, Defendt., als exo.

    - Ordered that MARY SPOO be payd by RICHARD WASHBURNE for seven days attendance according to Act being by him subpaened as an Evidence in the suite betweene the sd. RICHARD and JAMES TRENT, Defendt., als. exo.

    - Ordered that FRANCIS TERRETT be paid by RICHARD WASHBURNE for seven days attendance according to Act being by him subpaened as an Evidence in the suite between the said RICHARD and JAMES TRENT, Defendt., als exo.

- Ordered that THOMAS PATTY be paid by RICHARD WASHBURNE for seven days attendance according to Act being by him subpaened as an evidence in the suite betweene the said RICHARD, Plt. JAMES TRENT, Defendt., als exo.

p.   Richmond County Court 7th of December 1704
23   - Ordered that WILLIAM SIMMS be paid by RICHARD WASHBURNE for seven days attendance according to Act being by him subpaened as an evidence in the suite betweene the said RICHARD, Plt. and JAMES TRENT, Defendt., als exo.

- This day EDMOND McGLYNCHA, MARY SPOO, FRANCIS TERRETT, THOMAS PATTY and WILLIAM SIMMS came into Court and assigned theire rights of the Order obtained by them against the said RICHARD WASHBURNE as evidences for their attendance in the suite between the said RICHARD, Plt. and JAMES TRENT, Defendt., to him the said RICHARD

- Ordered that the Jury be paid theire charges in the suite between RICHD. WASHBURNE, Plt. and JAMES TRENT, Defendt.

- Certificate according to Act of Assembly is granted to Lieut. Coll. SAMLL. PEACHEY for five hundred acres of Land for Importation of ten persons into this Collony, by name,

WILLIAM POWELL	EDWARD CARVIN	DENNIS MOOREING
JENNY CUMMIN	ELINOR (U——)	JAMES PARRY
JOHN (H——)	ALICE TINSLEY	(G——) HARRIMAN
JO; DIXON		

the said SAMLL. makeing Oath that neither he nor any to his knowledge had received Certificate for the same, the Right of which he assigned in Court to Mr. EDWARD BARROW

- Certificate according to Act of Assembly is granted to WILLIAM HARWOOD for two hundred and fifty acres of land for Importation of five persons into this Collony by name, BRIDGET WHITE, TIMOTHY DAYLY, MARGRETT CLANCY, DUNCAN STEWARD DENICE (M——), the sd. WILLIAM makeing Oath that neither he nor any to his knowledge had received Certificate for the same, the Right of which he assigned in Court to Mr. EDWARD BARROW

- The action brought by ABRAHAM MARSHALL, Blacksmith, against ROBERT REYNOLDS, is dismist, the Plt. not prosecuting

- Especiall Imparlance is granted in the suite between JOHN WHITE and MARGARETT his Wife, Plts., and JOHN SIMMONS, Defendt. till next Court

- The Attachment granted last Court to JAMES PHILLIPS against the Estate of JOHN BROWNE is continued till next Court

- The action brought by JOHN CHARTRIS, Merchant, against FRANCIS LYNCH, Mercht., is dismist, the Plt. not prosecuting

- Nonsuite is granted to JOHN POUND against JOHN CHARTRIS there being no cause of action, and it is ordered that the said JNO: CHARTRIS pay the same together with costs of suite als exo.

- RICHARD APPLEBY, FRANCIS LUCAS, TIMOTHY DALY and STEPHEN DALY some of the Grand Jury of this County who failing to appeare with the rest to give in theire presentments it is ordered that each of them severally be fined the summe of two hundred pounds of tobbo. & yt. they pay the same wth: costs, &c.

p.   Richmond County Court 7th of December 1704
24   - The Citation brought by JOB HAMMOND, JUNR. and AMADINE his Wife,
        Admrx. of the Estate of THOMAS BAYLIS, deced., against JAMES SUG-
GITT, Defendt. is dismist, it being the oppinion of the Court that the sd. Citation was
not well brought
        - Ordered that RICHARD FOWLER be payd by ABRAHAM MARSHALL for
ten days attendance according to Act being by him subpaened as an evidence in the
suite betweene the said ABRAHAM, Plt. and ROBERT REYNOLDS, Defendt., als
exo.
        - The action brought by Majr. WILLIAM ROBINSON, agt. NEHEMIAH
JONES is continued till the next Court att the Plt.'s request
        - In the motion of Case betweene SYMON PASCOE, Plt. and THOMAS
HARPER, Defendt. for (this entry is not completed)
        - The action brought by Capt. JOHN TARPLEY, Assignee of ROBERT COLE,
agt. HENRY PERRY is dismist, the Plt. not prosecuting
        - The action of Debt betweene ROBERT JORDAN, Plt and WILLIAM LYN-
TON, Defendt., for two thousand five hundred fifty seven pounds of tobbo. by Accot.,
the said Defendt. being called and not appeareing nor any security returned, Judgment thereof is granted to the Plt. against the said Defendt. for the said summe of two
thousand five hundred and fifty seven pounds of tobbo. unless the sd. Defendt.
appeare att the next Court and answer the said action
        - Judgment being this day past against the Sheriff for two thousand five hun-
dred and fifty seven pounds of tobbo. unto ROBERT JORDAN for the non appeareance of WILLIAM LYNTON att the suite of the said ROBERT, upon the motion of
the Sheriff an Attachment is granted unto him against the Estate of the said WIL-
LIAM LYNTON for the summe aforesaid returnable to the next Court for Judgment.
        - The action brought by JOHN MASON against HENRY JOHN NEW-
BURNE is dismist, the Plt. not prosecuting
        - The action brought by BENJAMINE DEVERELL against GEORGE
WHITE is dismist, the Plt. not prosecuting
        - The action brought by BENJAMINE DEVERELL against ANDREW HAR-
RISON is dismist, the Plt. not prosecuting
        - Judgment upon Attachment is grented to WILLIAM PANNELL against the
Estate of WILLIAM ROBINSON for one thousand five hundred and fifty seven
pounds of tobbo. attached in the hands of the said Plt.the same being due by Bill
under the hand of the Defendt. and by Accot. proved by the Oath of the Plt.

p.   Richmond County Court 7th of December 1704
25   which is ordered to be paid wth: costs of suite als exo.
        - Judgment upon Attachment is granted to JAMES INGO against the Estate
of HENRY SALKELD for seven hundred and eighty pounds of tobbo. due by Accot.,
one hhd. of tobbo. being attached as part thereof in the tobbo. house of RICHARD
(B-----), wch: is ordered to be paid wth: costs of suite als exo.
        - Ordered that AVERY NAYLER do pay unto the Church Wardens of Sitten-
bourne Parish for the use of the sd. Parish the summe of five shillings Sterl. being the
Fine for hanging tobbo. on the Sabbath Day als exo.
        - JOHN REYNOLDS being summoned by last Court's Order to appeare att
this Court to give Bond to save harmless and keep indemnified the Church Wardens

of St. Mary's Parish for or by reason of a bastard Child layd to him by MARGARETT LAMB and fayling to appeare accordingly ordered that the Sheriff of this County or his Deputy do take him into safe Custody and him haveing taken to keep till he shall give sufficient security for his appeareance att the next Court

- The presentment of the Grand Jury against JOHN CAREY & CATHERINE OBLIN for goeing to bed together as man and wife is dismist

- Ordered that DANIELL McCARTY do returne Inventory and Appraisment of DARBY INGLISHBY's Estate to the next Court

- Judgment is granted to JAMES PHILLIPS againt HONOR WOFFENDALL, Exrx. of ADAM WOFFENDALL, for foure hundred pounds of tobbo. and caske convenient to water in Richmond County due by Bill wch: is ordered to be payd wth: costs of suite als exo.

- Judgment is granted to JOHN WORDEN agaisnt FRANCIS WILLIAMS for one thousand & fifty pounds of tobbo. and caske convenient in Richmond County due upon balla. of a Bill wch: is ordered to be payd wth: costs of suite als exo.

- This day JOHN JONES, Shoemaker, confest Judgment to JOHN WORDEN for five hundred and thirty pounds of tobbo. due by Accot. proved by the Oath of the Plt., which is ordered to be paid with costs of suite als exo.

- The action brought by HONOR WOFFENDALL, Exrx. of ADAM WOFFEN-DALL, is dismist, there being no cause of action

- The action brought by SAMLL. BAYLY against GEORGE BRUCE is dismist

- The action brought by ROBERT MOSELEY against JOHN BIRKETT is dismist, the Plt. not prosecuting

p.   Richmond County Court 7th of December 1704
26   - In an action of Debt betweene JOHN WORDEN, Plt. and RICHARD WIS-
        DELL, Defendt., for eight hundred and thirty two pounds of tobbo. by Accot.,
Judgment being granted the last Court against the Sheriff for the said summe unless the said Defendt. should appeare this Court and answer the said action, and the said Defendt. failing to appeare, it is therefore ordered that Capt. CHARLES BARBER, Sheriff of this County, pay unto the said JOHN WORDEN the said summe of eight hundred and thirty two pounds of tobbo with costs als exo.

- Attachment to the Sheriff for eight hundred and thirty two pounds of tobbo. against ye Estate of RICHARD WISDELL continued

- In an action of Case betweene JOHN WORDEN, Plt. and KATHERINE HENDERKIN, Defendt. for seven hundred and twenty foure pounds of tobbo convenient to water in Richmond County, Judgment being granted the last Court against the Sheriff for the said summe unless the said Defendt. should appeare att this Court and answer the said action, and the said Defendt. failing to appeare, it is therefore ordered that Capt. CHARLES BARBER, Sheriff of this County, do pay unto the said JOHN WORDEN the said summe of seven hundred and twenty foure pounds of tobbo. wth: costs als exo.

- Judgment upon Attachment is granted to Capt. CHARLES BARBER, Sheriff of this County, against the Estate of KATHERINE HENDERKIN for seven hundred and twenty foure pounds of tobbo. convenient to water in Richmond County, which is ordered to be paid wth: costs of suite als exo.

- The action brought by SAMLL. BAYLY against DAVID YOUNG is continued till next Court

- The action brought by JAMES INGO against JAMES PHILLIPS is dismist, the Plt. not prosecuting
- The action brought by THOMAS WHITE against THOMAS DEACUS is continued till the next Court
- This day WILLIAM SMITH, Cordwainer, confest Judgment to THOMAS WHITE for foure hundred and ninety five pounds of tobbo. in caske, wch: is ordered to be payd wth: costs of suite als exo.
- In ye action of Case betweene THOMAS WHITE & ROBERT PAYNE for foure hundred and eighty seven pounds of tobacco, the Defendt. not appeareing, Attachment is therefore granted to the said THOMAS WHITE against the Estate of ROBERT PAYNE returnable to next Court for Judgmt.
- The Attachment granted last Court to THOMAS WHITE against the Estate of GERRARD NEWTON is continued till next Court
- This day HONOR WOFFENDALL confest Judgment to THOMAS WHITE for two hundred and thirty two pounds of tobbo. wch: is ordered to be payd wth: costs of suite als exo.

p.   <u>Richmond County Court 7th of December 1704</u>
27
- The action brought by WILLIAM STONE, Assignee of JAMES PHILLIPS, against WILLIAM BOWLIN is dismist, the Plt. not prosecuting
- The action brought by ANTHONY SEALE against ROBERT LEGG is dismist, the Plt. not prosecuting
- In an action of Case betweene EDWARD NEWTON, Plt., and JAMES GRAHAM, Defendt., for Defendt. beating cursing and verily (In--------) SHILAH NEWTON, the Wife of the Plt., the Defendt. by his Atto. last Court haveing pleaded Not Guilty a Jury being this Court impannelled and sworne to try the matter in issue,

by name GEORGE GLASCOCK	WILLIAM FITZHERBERT	RAWLEIGH DOWNEMAN
JAMES SUGGITT	JOHN SIMONS	JOHN DALTON
JOHN MILLS	JOHN INGO	JAMES INGO
WILLIAM PANNELL	JOHN KELLY &	FRANCIS WILLIAMS

who being returned brought in the following Verdict; We of the Jury do find for the Defendt., which Verdict upon the motion of the Defendt. is ordered to be recorded, and that the said suite be dismist
- Especiall Imparlance granted in the suite betweene THOMAS WHITE, Plt. and JOHN DALTON, Defendt., till next Court
- The action brought by ANDREW CROMWELL and Capt. ROBERT McCARRELL of the Kingdome of Ireland against JOHN DALTON and MARY his Wife, Admrx. of WILLIAM BROCKENBROUGH, deced., is dismist, the Plts. not prosecuting
- Judgment is granted THOMAS MACKEY against JOHN DALTON for six hundred pounds of tobbo. which is ordered to be paid wth: costs of suite als exo.
- Especiall Imparlance is granted in the suite between THOMAS MACKEY, Plt. and THOMAS WHITE, Defendt., till next Court
- Judgment is granted to JAMES INGO against JOHN DALTON for five hundred pounds of tobbo. in caske due by Bill which is ordered to be paid wth: costs of suite als exo.
- Judgment renewed by Scire Facias to SEM COX against JOHN DALTON for foure hundred and sixty two pounds of tobbo. wch: is ordered to be payd wth: all for-

mer & present costs als exo.

- The action brought by HENRY SEGAR against THOMAS GLADMAN is dismist, the Plt. not prosecuting

- In an action of Debt betweene THOMAS GLOVER, Plt. and PETER OBLEN Defendt., for one thousand one hundred and seventy pounds of tobbo. by Accot., the Sheriff haveing returned the Defendt. non est inventus and not appeareing, Attachment is therefore granted to the Plt. against the Estate of the said Defendt. for the said summe of one thousand one hundred nd seventy pounds of tobbo. returnable to the next Court for Judgment

p.   Richmond County Court 7th of December 1704
28   - In an action of Debt betweene PATRICK CALLAHAN, Plt. and THOMAS
       GLADMAN, Defendt. for five hundred pounds of tobbo. in caske due by Bill, the
Defendt. being returned by the Sheriff non est inventus and failing to appeare, Attachment is therefore granted to the Plt. against the Estate of the said Defendt. for the said summe of five hundred pounds of tobbo. returnable to the next Court for Judgment

- The action brought by JOHN LOYD, Esqr., as well for an on behalfe of our Sovereigne Lady the Queene as for and on behalfe of himselfe against JOHN CHAMP is dismist, the Plt. not prosecuting

- The action brought by SAMLL. SAMFORD against FRANCIS LYNCH is dismist, the Plt. not prosecuting

- This day PATRICK CALLAHAN confest Judgment to AVERY NAYLER for six hundred and nine pounds of tobbo. in caske due by Bill, wch: is ordered to be paid wth: costs of suite als exo.

- In an action of Debt between CHARLES SMITH, Plt. and PETER OBLIN, Defendt., the Defendt. being returned by the Sheriff non est inventus and failing to appeare, Attachment is therefore granted to the Plt. against the Estate of the said Defendt. for five hundred and fifteene pounds of tobbo., the same being due by Bill, retunable to the next Court for Judgmt.

- The action brought by JAMES KITCHEN against MARTIN FISHER is dismist, the Plt. not prosecuting

- Especiall Imparlance is granted in the suite betweene WILLIAM HARWOOD, Plt., and JOSHUA LAWSON, Defendt. till next Court

- The action brought by GEORGE WHITE against HENRY BRADLEY is dismist, the Plt. not prosecuting

- The action brought by JAMES STIGELEER against JOHN HAWKINS is dismist, the Plt. not prosecuting

- In an action of Debt between AVERY NAYLER, Plt. and GEORGE RADFORD, Defendt. for five hundred and forty five pounds of tobbo. due by Bill to be paid upon the Plantation of the Defendt., and the Defendt. being called and not appeareing, Judgment is therefore granted to the Plt. against JOHN KINER, Security returned for his appeareance for the said summe unless the Defendt. appeare att the next Court and answer the sd. action

p.   Richmond County Court 7th of December 1704
29   - The action brought by EDWARD JEFFREYS against MORGAN SWYNEY

is dismist, the Plt. not prosecuting

- The action brought by THOMAS GREGSON against MORGAN SWYNEY is dismist, the Plt. not prosecuting

- The action brought by GARRARD NEWTON against DANIELL MERRITT is dismist, the Plt. not prosecuting

- The action brought by AVERY NAYLER against JOHN HEWS is dismist, the Plt. not prosecuting

- In an action of Case betweene JOHN GREENE, Plt. and ANTHONY SEALE, Defendt., for six hundred pounds of tobbo., and the Defendt. being called and not appeareing nor any security returned, Judgment is therefore granted to the Plt. against the Defendt. for the summe aforesaid unless the Defendt. appeare att the next Court and answer the said action

- Judgment being this day past against the Sheriff for six hundred pounds of tobbo. to JOHN GREENE for the non appeareance of ANTHONY SEALE, att the suite of the said JOHN, upon the motion of the Sheriff an Attachment is granted unto him against the Estate of ANTHONY SEALE for the summe aforesaid, returnable to the next Court

- The action brought by THOMAS OSBORNE against MAURICE HAMLETT is dismist, the Plt. not prosecuting

- The action brought by CHARLES WALKER against MAURICE HAMLETT is dismist, the Plt. not prosecuting

- The action brought by HERBERT (————) of Lyn Regis in the County of Norfolk in the Kingdom of England, Merchant, Admr. of WM. CLARKE, Mercht., deced., against MAURICE HAMLETT is dismist, the Plt. not prosecuting

- The action brought by WILLIAM BARBER and JOYCE his Wife against SAMLL. SAMFORD is dismist, the Plts. not prosecuting

- In an action of Case betweene JOHN TARPLEY, Plt. and THOMAS MACKEY, Defendt. for two pounds, seven shillings and eight pence due by Accot., the Defendt. being returned by the Sheriff non est inventus and not appeareing, Attachment is therefore granted to the Plt. against the Defendt. for the summe aforesaid returnable to the next Court for Judgmt.

- The action brought by HENRY BRERETON against ELIZA: LYNCH, Admrx. of STEPHEN LYNCH, is continued till next Court

- In an action of Case betweene PHEBE SLAUGHTER, Plt. and HENRY HAYES, Defendt. for 600 pounds of tobbo. the Defendt. being returned by the Sheriff non est inventus and not appeareing, Attachment is therefore granted the Plt. against the Estate of the Defendt. for the summe aforesd., returnable to the next Court for Judgment

p.   Richmond County Court 7th of December 1704

30   - The action brought by JAMES CAWARD against THOMAS LOYD is dismist, the Plt. not prosecuting

- The action brought by ELIZABETH HOWELL, against JOHN ALLOWAY and WILLIAM SMITH, Admrs. of the Estate of JOHN HOWELL, deced., is dismist, the Plt. not haveing any cause for action

- Richmond County is Dr. to the severall Claymes hereafter mentioned, vizt.

To Majr. WILLIAM ROBINSON for expenses and his man's	4839
To THOMAS LEWIS for keeping TOTUSKEY FERRY	5000
To RICHARD SHIPPEY	0440
To ROBERT PAYNE	0440
To THOMAS WHITE	0440
To JOHN RENELLS	0440
To ADAM WOFFENDALL	0440
To JAMES STROTHER	0440
To JAMES PORTER	0600
To MARK RYMER	0600
To THOMAS PHILIPIN	0600
To WILLIAM ROWLAND	0600
To WILLIAM STONE	0600
To JAMES RICHARDSON	0600
To JOHN CORBIN	0600
To WILLIAM BALLARD	3560
To WILLIAM ROBERTSON	1345
To JAMES SHERLOCK, Clk. of Richmd. County	1080
To Mr. Secretary's fees	0190
To JAMES SHERLOCK, Clk., for attending att a Called Court	0200
To SEM COX for a Wolf's head	0200
To Capt. CHARLES BARBER, Sherriff R. C.	0500
To GARRARD LYNCH, Under Sherriff, R. C.	0500
To WILLIAM LAMBERT for a Wolf's head	0200
To PHILLIP HARRIS for six Wolves' heads	1200
To JOHN HARRIS for five Wolves' heads	1000
To 3 Tythables Runaway allowed to JAMES INGO.	0090
To 3 Tythables runaway allowed to SAMLL. BAYLY	0090

Richmond County Court 7th of December 1704

p.
31

To Capt. WILLIAM UNDERWOOD for one Inquest	0199
To DAVID JACKSON for keeping the Beaverdam's cutt	0100
To EDWARD JEFFREYS for cleansing the Court House and finding a Lock and a Staple for the Doore wch: he assigned to Colo. GEO: TAYLER	0540
To Colo. GEORGE TAYLER for one Inquest	0133
To JOHN KELLY for makeing a Bridge over RAPPA: CREEKE and his expenses about it	0500
To Sallary for 27800 att 10 p cent	2780
To Caske for 2780 att 8 p cent	2224
To the Fraction given to CHARLES BARBER, Sherriff	0570
	31374

- Ordered that Capt. CHARLES BARBER, High Sherriff of this County or his Deputy do collect twenty one pounds of tobbo. p poll for every Tithable person within this County and out thereof do pay unto every respective person all the summes herein contained and in case any person or persons shall refuse payment thereof, that the said CHARLES BARBER or his Deputy do make distress for the same and for he or theire soe doeing this shall be a sufficient warrant

- Upon the motion of SAMLL. BAYLY and JAMES INGO, late Under Sherriffs of this County, Order is granted them to claime for all areareages of Publick Dues not collected by them the last yeare

- Ordered that THOMAS LEWIS do continue keeping TOTUSKEY FERRY and that he receive the same att the next laying of the levy the summe of five thousand pounds of tobbo.

p.   - Att a Court held for Richmond County the 7th day of February 1704
32   Present
       Lieut. Colo. GEORGE TAYLER   Capt. JOHN TARPLEY
       Lieut. Colo. SAMLL. PEACHEY   Majr. WM. ROBINSON   Justices

- This day JOHN CHAMP acknowledged the Assignment of Deeds of Lease and Release for Land wth: Bond to JOHN WRIGHT, which is ordered to be recorded
- This day GEORGE ESKRIDGE, Attorney for and on the behalfe of JOHN BROWNE, acknowledged a Deed for Land to JAMES LOUGHAN which is ordered to be recorded
- Upon the Petition of JAMES INGO, ordered that the Division of Land proposed by him to this Court be recorded
- This day JAMES INGO acknowledged a Deed for Land wth: Bond to GEORGE GLASCOCK, wch: is ordered to be recorded
- Upon the Petition of EDWARD MOZINGO, ordered that the Eare marke of his hoggs and cattle, being a swallow forke on the left eare and a hole on the right eare be recorded
- Upon the Petition of EDWARD MOZINGO, JUNR., ordered that the Eare marke of his hoggs and cattle, being a swallow forke on the right eare and a cropp on the left eare be recorded
- Upon the Petition of HENRY WILSON, ordered that the Eare marke of his hoggs and cattle, being a crop and two slitts on the right Eare and two under keeles on the left eare be recorded
- This day STEPHEN GUBTON acknowledged a Deed for Land to GEORGE GLASCOCK wch: is ordered to be recorded
- The Probate of the Last Will and Testament of JAMES SUGGITT continued till next Court
- The Probate of the Last Will and Testament of JAMES SAMFORD continued till next Court
- Upon the motion of Madam KATHERINE GWYN, Widdo. & Relict of Majr. DAVID GWYN, late of this County, deced., the Order granted to her

p.   Richmond County Court 7th of February 1704/1705
33   last Court for laying out and separating her joynture from the Estate of the
       said Majr. DAVID GWYN, is continued till next Court; And it is ordered that
Colo. WILLIAM TAYLOE, Capt. JOHN TARPLEY, Capt. THOMAS BEALE and JAMES SHERLOCK or any three of them do meet att the House of the said Majr. DAVID GWYN some time betweene this and the next Court and do then & there lay out and separate the joynture of the said Madm. KATHERINE GWYN's from the Estate of the said Majr. DAVID GWYN, according to the intent and purport of the last Court Order and make report of theire proceedings therein to the next Court under theire hands in writing
- The Order for GARRARD LYNCH to give Bond for the tutoridge of SAMLL INGLISHBY, Son of DARBY INGLISHBY, continued till next Court

- The presentment of the Grand Jury of this County against WILLIAM CAM-BELL upon suspition of his liveing in adultery wth: MARY RICHARDSON is continued upon condition that he give security att the next Court for his good behaviour in that respect and upon failure or contempt thereof, it is ordered that the Sherriff of this County or his Deputy do take him into safe custody and him to detaine till he shall give Bond wth: sufficient security for the refraineing the company of the said MARY RICHARDSON

- WILLIAM WOODBRIDGE appeareing att this Court to answer the presentment of the Grand Jury against him upon suspition of his living in adultery wth: the Wife of ZACHARIAH NICHOLLS, and being admonished thereof, ordered that unless the said WILLIAM WOODBRIDGE do refrayne the company of the said ZACHARIAH NICHOLLS his Wife, he be summoned by the Sherriff of this County to the next Court there to give Bond wth: security for his good behaviour in that respect for the future

- ABRAHAM DALE being summoned to this Court to answer the presentment of the Grand Jury against him for goeing to look for Deer Skins on the Sabbath Day, and not appeareing, ordered that he be fined according to Law and that he pay the same wth: costs als exo.

- GILBERT CROSSWELL being summoned to this Court to answer the presentment of the Grand Jury against him for travelling on the Sabbath Day and not appeareing, ordered that he be fined according to Law and that he pay the same with costs als exo.

p.   Richmond County Court 7th of February 1704/1705
34   - RICHARD WHITE being summoned to this Court to answer the presentment of the Grand Jury against him for Drinking and makeing merry att his House on the Sabbath Day wth; JOHN BROWNE and CORNELIUS HARKIN and not appeareing, ordered that he be fined according to Law and that he pay the same wth: costs als exo.

- ALEXANDER CAMMELL being summoned to this Court to answer the presentment of the Grand Jury against him for carrying a Gunn in the Woods on the Sabbath Day, and failing to appeare, ordered that he be fined according to Law and that he pay the same wth: costs als exo.

- RICHARD SMITH being summoned to this Court to answer the presentment of the Grand Jury against him for not goeing to Church for two moneths together, and not appeareing, ordered that he be fined according to Law and that he pay the same wth: costs also exo.

- PETER ELMORE being summoned to this Court to answer the presentment of the Grand Jury against him for not goeing to Church for two moneths together and failing to appeare, ordered that he be fined according to Law and that he pay the same wth: costs als exo.

- THOMAS DURHAM being summoned to this Court to answer the presentment of the Grand Jury against him for not goeing to Church for two moneth together and not appeareing, ordered that he be fined according to Law and that he pay the same wth: costs als exo.

- The presentment of the Grand Jury against JOHN OLDHAM for not goeing to Church for two moneths together is dismist, the said JOHN makeing appeare to the contrary

- JOHN HANCOCK being summoned to appeare att this Court to answer the presentment of the Grand Jury against him for not goeing to Church for two moneths together and not appeareing, ordered that he be fined according to Law and that he pay the same wth: costs als exo.

- GEORGE DEVENPORT being summoned to this Court to answer the presentment of the Grand Jury against him for not goeing to Church for two moneths together and failing to appeare, ordered that he be fined according to Law and that he pay the same wth: costs als exo.

- PHILLIP HARRIS being summoned to this Court to answer the presentment of the Grand Jury against him for not goeing to Church for two moneth together and now appeareing, ordered that he be fined according to Law and that he pay the same wth: costs als exo.

p.   Richmond County Court 7th of February 1704/1705
35   - JOHN TINTOR being summoned to this Court to answer the presentment of the Grand Jury against him for not goeing to Church for two moneths together, and not appeareing, ordered that he be fined according to Law and that he pay the same wth: costs als exo.

- STEPHEN GUBTON being summoned to this Court to answer the presentment of the Grand Jury against him for not goeing to Church for two moneths together, and not appeareing, ordered that he be fined according to Law and that he pay the same wth: costs als exo.

- PETER ELLIS JUNR., being summoned to answer the presentment of the Grand Jury against him for not goeing to Church for two moneths together and failing to appeare, ordered that he be fined according to Law and that he pay the same wth: costs als exo.

- JOSHUA STONE being summoned to this Court to answer the presentment of the Grand Jury against him for not goeing to Church for two moneths together & not appeareing, ordered that he be fined according to Law and that he pay the same wth: costs als exo.

- CHARLES DODSON, JUNR. being summoned to this Court to answer the presentment of the Grand Jury against him for not goeing to Church for two moneths together and not appeareing, ordered that he be fined according to Law and that he pay the same with costs als exo.

- THOMAS DODSON being summoned to this Court to answer the presentment of the Grand Jury against him for not goeing to Church for two moneths together and not appeareing, ordered that he be fined according to Law and that he pay the same with costs als exo.

- SAMUELL JONES being summoned to this Court to answer the presentment of the Grand Jury against him for not goeing to Church for two moneth together and not appeareing, ordered that he be fined according to Law and that he pay the same wth: costs als exo

- JOHN ROBERTS being summoned to this Court to answer the presentment of the Grand Jury against him for not goeing to Church for two moneths together and not appeareing, ordered that he be fined according to Law and that he pay the same wth: costs of suit als exo.

- EDMUND OVERTON being summoned to this Court to answer the presentment against him for not goeing to Church for two moneths together and not appeareing, ordered that he be fined according to Law and that he pay the same wth: costs als exo.

p.   Richmond County Court 7th of February 1704-1705
36   THOMAS SHERLOCK being summoned to this Court to answer the present-
        ment of the Grand Jury against him for not goeing to Church for two moneths
together and not appeareing, ordered that the be fined according to Law and that he pay the same wth: costs als exo.
        - GILBERT CROSSWELL being summoned to this Court to answer the pre-
sentment of the Grand Jury against him for not goeing to Church for two moneths together and not appeareing, ordered that he be fined according to Law and that he pay
the same wth: costs als exo.
        - JOHN RANKIN being summoned to this Court to answer the presentment
of the Grand Jury against him for not goeing to Church for two months together and
not appeareing, ordered that he be fined according to Law and that he pay the same
wth: costs als exo.
        - THOMAS MARTON being summoned to this Court to answer the present-
ment of the Grand Jury against him for not goeing to Church for two moneth together
and not appeareing, ordered that he be fined according to Law and that he pay the
same wth: costs als exo.
        - JAMES PEARSON being summoned to this Court to answer the present-
ment of the Grand Jury against him for not goeing to Church for two moneths together and not appeareing, ordered that he be fined according to Law and that he pay
the same wth: costs als exo.
        - The presentment of the Grand Jury against THOMAS NEWTON for not
going to Church for two moneths together is dismist, the said THOMAS not living in
this County
        - The presentment of the Grand Jury against ANDREW HARRISON for
turning out & tending seconds is continued and ordered tht the Sherriff of this County
or his Deputy do take him into Custody till he give security for his appeareance att
the next Court to answer the said presentment
        - WILLIAM SMITH, JUNR. being summoned to this Court to answer the pre-
sentment of the Grand Jury against him for fishing on the Sabbath Day & failing to
appeare, ordered that he be fined according to law and that he pay the same wth:
costs als exo.
        - CORNELIUS HARKIN being summoned to this Court to answer the pre-
sentment of the Grand Jury against him for not goeing to Church for two

p.   Richmond County Court 7th of February 1704/1705
37   moneths together did accordingly appeare but offering no matterial proofe
        against the presentment, ordered that he be fined according to Law and that he
pay the same wth: costs als exo.
        - RICHARD GREENE being summoned to this Court to answer the present-
ment of the Grand Jury against him for selling Rumm and Sugar on the Sabbath Day
did accordingly appeare but offering nothing matterial in barr of the said presentment
ordered that he be fined according to Law and that he pay the same wth: costs als exo
        - The presentment of the Grand Jury against ABRAHAM   HANNISON &

MARTHA NEWDALL for fornication is continued and ordered that the Sherriff of this County do take them into safe custody till they shall give security for theire appeareance att the next Court to answer the said presentment

- The presentment of the Grand Jury against ABRAHAM HANNISON for selling Sider of the Sabbath Day is continued and ordered that the Sherriff of this County or his Deputy do take him into safe custody and him to detaine until he shall give security for his appeareance att the next Court to answer the said presentment

- The presentment of the Grand Jury against WILLIAM RICHARDSON for hunting on the Sabbath Day is continued and ordered that the Sherriff of this County or his Deputy do take him into safe custody till he shall give security for his appeareance att the next Court to answer the said presentment

- The presentment of the Grand Jury against ROGER RICHARDSON for carrying a Gunn in the Woods on the Sabbath Day is continued and ordered that the Sherriff of this County or his Deputy do take him into safe custody till he shall give security for his appeareance att the next Court to answer the said presentment

- NICHOLAS SMITH being summoned to this Court to answer the presentment of the Grand Jury against him for selling Rumm on the Sabbath Day and he appeareing and offering no sufficient proofe to the contrary, ordered that he be fined according to Law and that he pay the same wth: costs als exo

- WILLIAM GRANT being summoned to appeare att this Court to answer the presentment of the Grand Jury against him for being Drunk on the Sabbath Day, who appeareing accordinlgy and offering no matterial proofe agt. the said presentment, ordered that he be fined according to Law and that he pay the same wth: costs als exo

p.   Richmond County Court 7th of February 1704/1705
38   - JOHN WARD being summoned to this Court to answer the presentment of
        the Grand Jury against him for being Drunk on the Sabbath Day did accordingly appeare and offering nothing matterial against the said presentment, ordered that he be fined according to Law and that he pay the same wth: costs also exo

- CHRISTOPHER EDRINGTON being summoned to this Court to answer the presentment of the Grand Jury against him for being Drunk on ye Sabbath Day did accordingly appeare but offering nothing matterial against the said presentment, ordered that he be fined according to Law and that he pay the same wth: costs als exo

- RICHARD PAYNE being summoned to this Court to answer the presentment of the Grand Jury against him for being Drunk on the Sabbath Day did accordingly appeare but offering nothing matterial against the said presentment, ordered that he be fined according to Law and that he pay the same wth: costs als exo

- OWEN McCARTY being summoned to this Court to answer the presentment of the Grand Jury against him for being Drunk on the Sabbath Day and offering nothing matterial against the said presentment, ordered that he be fined according to Law and that he pay the same wth: costs als exo

- STEPHEN NOWLIN being summoned to this Court to answer the presentment of the Grand Jury against him for being Drunk on the Sabbath Day and offering nothing matterial against the said presentment, ordered that he be fined according to Law and that he pay the same wth: costs als exo

- The presentment of the Grand Jury against CISELY JORDAN for suffering WILLIAM GRANT, JOHN WARD, CHRISTOPHER EDRINGTON, RICHARD

PAYNE, OWEN McCARTY & STEPHEN NOWLIN to drink sweare & sing att her House on the Sabbath Day is continued, and ordered that the Sherriff of this County or his Deputy do take her into custody till she shall give security for her appeareance att the next Court to answer the said presentment

- THOMAS NEWMAN being summoned to this Court to answer the presentment of the Grand Jury against him for being Drunk on ye Sabbath, and not appeareing, ordered that he be fined according to Law and that he pay the same wth: costs als exo

- The presentment of the Grand Jury against WILLIAM HILL for fishing on the Sabbath Day is continued till next Court and ordered that the Sherriff of this County or his Deputy do take him (this entry is not completed)

p. 39   Richmond County Court 7th of February 1704/1705
- The presentment of the Grand Jury against ABRAHAM GOAD's Servant woman for burying her bastard Child privately is continued till next Court and ordered that THOMAS FERRELL and JOHN WALLIS be summoned to the next Court to give theire evidence relating to the buriall of the Child

- This day ABRAHAM GOAD acknowledged himselfe security for the appeareance of his Servant woman att the next Court to answer the presentment of the Grand Jury against her for burying her bastard Child privately.

- Capt. JOHN TARPLEY certifying to this Court tht JOHN OLDHAM had given security for saveing harmeless the Parish of Northfarnham of and from all charges & incumbrances that may arise or acrew for or by reason of a Child named BRYAN BREEDING, aged three yeares old the 15th day of October last. Ordered that the said BRYAN BREEDING do live with JOHN OLDHAM or his assignes till he shall arrive to the age of twenty one yeares

- This day JOHN DALTON confest Judgment to THOMAS WHITE for fifteene hundred and eighty pounds of tobbo. wch: is ordered to be paid wth: costs of suite als exo

- Upon the Petition of WILLIAM HANKS, Order for administration is granted him on all and singular the Estate of his deced. Father, WILLIAM HANKS, he giving security according to Law

- This day Capt. JNO: TARPLEY and JOHN SIMMONS acknowledged themselves indebted to the Worspll. her Majties. Justices for Richmond County in the full and just summe of twenty thousand pounds of tobbo & caske to be paid to the said Justices, Exrs. & Admrs. in case WM. HANKS do not duely administer all and singular the Estate of his deced., Father, WM. HANKS, and surrender up the same when thereunto lawfully called

- Ordered by this Court that a Court of Claymes be held att the Courthouse of this County on the Tuesday before the next Court

- The Court is adjourned till ye first Wednesday in March

p. 40   Att a Court of Claymes held att Richmond County Courthouse the 6th day of March 1704   Present
Lieut. Colo. GEORGE TAYLER   Capt. JNO: TARPLEY
Capt. WILLIAM UNDERWOOD   Capt. THOMAS BEALE   Justices

- This day the Clayme of WILLIAM TAYLOE, Colo. and Commander in Cheife of this County in behalfe of himselfe &c. concerning the NANZATICO INDIANS, being presented to this Court and by them examined, the same was accordingly allowed of and ordered to be recorded

   - This day the Clayme of Capt. CHARLES BARBER, Sherriff of this County concerning the NANZATICO INDIANS being by him presented to this Court and the same by them examined was by the allowed of and ordered to be recorded

   - This day the Clayme of THOMAS DICKENSON concerning the NANZATICO INDIANS being by him presented to this Court and by them examined, the same was accordingly allowed of and ordered to be recorded

   - This day Capt. CHARLES BARBER, Sherriff of this County, presenting to this Court his Account relateing to the NANZATICO INDIANS, the same being by them examined is allowed of according to Law

   - This day the Clayme of GARRARD LYNCH, Under Sherriff of Richmond County, being by him presented to this Court & the same by them examined, was accordingly allowed of and ordered to be recorded

   - This day the Clayme of MRS. JANE CAMMELL, Interpreter for the Tryall of the NANZATICO INDIANS being by her presented to this Court & by them examined was accordingly ordered to be recorded

   - This day the Clayme of NATHANLL. POPE, one of the Clks. of the Arraignment to the Commissioners of Oyer and Terminer for the Tryall of the NANZATICO INDIANS being by him presented to this court & by them examined, the same is accordingly allowed of and ordered to be recorded

   - This day the Clayme of JAMES SHERLOCK, one of the Clks, of the Arraignment to the Commissioners of Oyer and Terminer for the Tryall of the

p.   <u>Richmond County Court of Claymes 6th of March 1704/1705</u>
41   NANZATICO INDIANS being by him presented to this Court and by them examined, is accordingly allowed of and ordered to be recorded

   - The Court of Claymes adjourned till tomorrow morning att eight of the Clock

   - Att a Court of Claymes held at the Courthouse of Richmond County on the 7th day of March 1704   Present

Lieut. Colo. GEORGE TAYLER	Capt. JOHN TARPLEY
Lieut. Colo. SAMLL. PEACHEY	Capt. ALEXR: DONIPHAN
Capt. WM. UNDERWOOD	Capt. THOMAS BEALE
Capt. JOHN DEANE	Justices

   - This day the Clayme of Capt. WILLIAM UNDERWOOD in behalfe of himselfe & his Company being presented to the Court by him and the same by them perused is allowed of and ordered to be recorded

   - This day the Clayme of Capt. ALEXANDER DONIPHAN concerning the NANZATICO INDIANS being by him presented to the Court in behalfe of himselfe and his Company and by them examined, the same is accordingly allowed of and ordered to be recorded

   - This day the Clayme of RICHARD BUCKNER, one of the Clks. of the Arraignment to the Commissioners of Oyer and Terminer for the Tryall of the NANZATICO INDIANS being by him presented to this Court and the same by them examined, the same is accordingly allowed of and ordered to be recorded

- This day the Clayme of JAMES WESTCOMB, one of the Clks. of the Arraignment to the Commissioners of Oyer and Terminer for the Tryall of the NANZATICO INDIANS being by him presented to this Court and by them examined is accordingly allowed of and ordered to be recorded

- This day the Clayme of NICHOLAS SMITH in behalfe of himselfe and the Troops under his Command being by him presented to this Court & by them examined is accordingly allowed of and ordered to be recorded

p. 42   Att a Court held for Richmond County the 7th day of March 1704
Present

Lieut. Colo. GEORGE TAYLER   Capt. JOHN TARPLEY
Lieut. Colo. SAMLL. PEACHEY   Capt. ALEXANDER DONIPHAN
Capt. WILLIAM UNDERWOOD   Capt. THOMAS BEALE
Capt. JOHN DEANE   Justices

- JANE CUMMIN, Servant to Lieut. Colo. SAMLL. PEACHEY being presented to this Court by her said Master for committing the sin of fornication & having a bastard Child, ordered that the said JANE do serve her said Master or his assignes according to Act in compensation for the trouble of his House dureing the time of her Childbirth

- This day the Last Will and Testament of AVERY NAYLER being presented to this Court by the Exrx. therein named for proofe, the same was proved by the Oaths of SEABURN PINCHETT, JAMES MURPHY & STEPHEN HUCISON, wittnesses thereto and order for Probate granted thereon

- This day Lieut. Colo. SAMLL. PEACHEY confest Judgment to the Church Wardens of Northfarnham Parish for the use of the said Parish for five hundred pounds of tobbo., being the fine of JANE CUMMIN for committing the sin of fornication and having a bastard Child

- Ordered that JANE CUMMIN by and with her owne consent do serve her Master, Lieut. Colo. SAMLL. PEACHEY or his assignes, the terme of fourteene moneths after her time by Indenture custome or otherwise be fully expired in compensation for his paying her fine for committing the sin of fornication and having a bastard Child

- Capt. JOHN TARPLEY certifying to the Court that Lieut. Colo. SAMLL. PEACHEY had made information on the first day of Febry. last before him against EDWARD POWELL for the said EDWARD's stealing of hogg from the said SAMLL. PEACHEY, & the said EDWARD being by his owne confession convicted of the aforesaid crime, Judgment is therefore granted unto the said SAMLL. PEACHEY against the said EDWARD POWELL for two yeares service according to Act of Assembly in that case made and provided

- This day DANLL. McCARTY, Attorney for and on the behalfe of SAMLL.

p. 43   Richmond County Court 7th of March 1704/1705
SAMFORD, acknowledged Deeds of Lease and Release for land to SARAH KEENE, wch: are ordered to be recorded

- ELIZABETH SAMFORD, Wife of the said SAMLL. SAMFORD, acknowledged her Right of Inheritance to the said land wch: is likewise ordered to be recorded

- This day JOHN INGO acknowledged a Deed for land with Bond to GEORGE

GLASCOCK which is ordered to be recorded

    - DANLL. McCARTY, Attorney of MARTHA INGO, relinquished her Right of Dower in the said Land

    - This day the Lre. of Attorney made by MARTHA INGO to DANLL. McCARTY was proved by the Oath of JOHN SYMMONS and ordered to be recorded

    - This day WILLIAM PHILLIPS came into Court and acknowledged that he was willing to serve WILLIAM HANKS the terme of seven yeares, he the said WILLIAM oblidging himselfe to do his uttermost endeavour to teach the said WILLIAM PHILLIPS the Trade of a Carpenter and help to find him, the said WILLIAM, sufficient dyett and cloathing and att the expiration thereof to give him a new suite of Broad Cloath and a sett of Carpenter's tools

    - This day JOSEPH BEALE acknowledged a Deed for Land with Bond to LUKE THORNTON, JUNR., wch: is ordered to be recorded

    - This day SYMON TAYLER, CHRISTOPHER PRIDHAM and THOMAS JESPER acknowledged a Deed for Land to JOSEPH DEEKE and WILLIAM LYNTON wch: is ordered to be recorded

    - Upon the motion of WILLIAM HANKS, ordered that ROWLAND LAWSON, WILLIAM SMOOT, DOM: BENEHAN & THOMAS BRYAN or any three of them some time betweene this and the next Court do meet att the House of the said WILLIAM HANKS and do then and there inventory and appraise all and singular the Estate of WILLIAM HANKS, deced., as shall be presented to their view and report of theire proceedings therein to the next Court under theire hands in writing. Capt. JOHN TARPLEY is requested to administer the Oaths to the Appraisers for theire true appraisment of the said deced.'s Estate as also to the Admr. for the true delivery thereof

    - This day the Inventory and Appraisment of the Estate of DARBY INGLISHBY, deced., was presented to this Court by SAMLL. BAYLY, the same is ordered to be recorded

    - Upon the Petition of TIMOTHY ICK, Servant to JAMES SCOTT, for his Freedome, ordered that unless the said JAMES SCOTT appeare att the next Court and answer the Complaint of the said TIMOTHY that the sd. TIMOTHY be free and acquitted from the service of the said JAMES SCOTT

p.   Richmond County Court 7th of March 1794/1705
44   - This day DANLL. McCARTY, Admr. of the Estate of DARBY INGLISHBY, deced., exhibitting an Accot. against the Estate of the said deced., and makeing Oath that the same was due from the said Estate, the same is by he Court allowed of and ordered to be recorded

    - This day SAMLL. BAYLY makeing Oath that there was two hundred & twenty eight pounds of tobbo. due unto him out of the Estate of DARBY INGLISHBY deced., as Clk. and Sherriff fees, the same is allowed of by this Court and ordered that he be paid ye same out of the Estate of the said deced., in the hands of DANLL. McCARTY, his Admr. als exo

    - Upon the presentment of the Grand Jury against KATHERINE THATCHELL, Servant to ABRAHAM GOAD for the buryall of her bastard Child privately, the said ABRAHAM makeing Oath tht the said Child was decayed & to the best of his Judgment still born and that he had taken it up some small time after the buryall thereof for which reason this Court do dismiss the said presentment & order that the said KATHERINE be discharged, but that she serve the said ABRAHAM according to Law for his paying all fees incident or due upon the said presentment after her time by Indenture custome or otherwise be fully expired

- This day ABRAHAM GOAD confest Judgmt. to the Church Wardens of Northfarnham Parish for the use of the said Parish, for five hundred pounds of tobbo. being the fine of KATHERINE THATCHELL for committing ye sin of fornication and having a bastard Child wth: costs als exo

- Ordered that KATHERINE THATCHELL by with with her owne consent do serve her Master, ALEXANDER GOAD, or his assignes, the terme of eight moneths after her time by Indenture custome or otherwise be fully expired in compensation for his paying of her fine for committing the sin of fornication and having a bastard Child

- Upon the Petition of JOHN HARPER, Order for Administration is granted to him on all and singular the Estate of WILLIAM HARPER, deced., he giving security according to Law

- This day Lieut. Colo. SAMLL. PEACHEY and Capt. JOHN TARPLEY acknowledged themselves indebted to the Worspll her Majties. Justices for Richmond County in the full and just summe of one hundred thousand pounds of good tobbo. and caske to be paid to the said Justices theire Exrs. and Admrs. in case JOHN HARPER do not duely administer

p.   Richmond County Court 7th of March 1704/1705
45   on all and singular the Estate of WILLIAM HARPER, deced., and render a
true Account thereof when he shall be thereunto lawfully called

- Pursuant to an Order of Court of the seventh of February last JAMES SHERLOCK returning to this Court the separation of the Joynture of Madm. KATHERINE GWYN, Widdo. and Relict of Majr. DAVID GWYN, deced, from the Estate of the sd. deced. according to one Deed of Joynture bearing date ye 28th of February 1680 and one certaine Schedule to the said Deed annexed, (the sheep, cattle, hoggs, mares & kitching utensills in the said Schedule mentioned not inserted in the said separation excepted) upon the motion of the said KATHERINE GWYN the same is ordered to be recorded

- The Probate of the Last Will & Testament of JOHN SUGGITT being continued by the Orders of December & February Courts last for the appeareance of ROBERT CLARKE, one of the wittnesses thereto & the same being proved in ye December Court by ye Oath of JAMES MURPHY (the other evidence) was this day proved by the Oath of the said ROBERT CLARKE and Order for Probate granted thereon

- The Probate of the Last Will and Testament of JAMES SAMFORD continued till next Court

- The presentment of the Grand Jury against WILLIAM CAMBELL upon his living in adultery with MARY RICHARDSON is continued till next Court

- The presentment of the Grand Jury against WILLIAM WOODBRIDGE upon his living in adultery with the Wife of ZACHARIAH NICHOLLS is dismist

- The presentment of the Grand Jury against ZACHARIAH NICHOLLS for living in adultery wth: MARY MALADY continued and ordered to give Bond

- This day ROBERT CLARKE acknowledged Bond for a Deed for Land to GEORGE ESKRIDGE which is ordered to be recorded

- The Court is adjourned for halfe an hour

Att a Court continued & held for Richmond County the 7th day of March 1704
Present

Lieut. Colo. GEORGE TAYLER   Capt. ALEXANDER DONIPHAN
Capt. JOHN DEANE   Capt. THOMAS BEALE
Capt. JOHN TARPLEY   Justices

- the Petition of Madm. KATHERINE GWYN for the administration of the Estate of PATRICK LAUGHEE, deced., is continued till next Court

p.   Att a Court held for Richmond County the 8th day of March 1704
46   Present
Lieut. Colo. GEORGE TAYLER   Capt. ALEXANDER DONIPHAN
Capt. WM. UNDERWOOD   Majr. WILLIAM ROBINSON Justices

- WILLIAM WOOD being summoned by the Sherriff to this Court to answer the presentment of the Grand Jury against him for not goeing to Church for two moneths together and not appeareing, ordered that he be fined for the same according to Law & that he pay the same wth: costs &c.
- DENNIS CAMERON being summoned by the Sherriff to answer the presentment of the Grand Jury against him for not goeing to Church for two moneths together and not appearing, ordered that he be fined according to Law and that he pay the same with costs &c.
- WILLIAM CAMBELL being summoned by the Sherriff to answer the presentment of the Grand Jury against him for not goeing to Church for two moneths together and not appeareing, ordered that he be fined according to Law and that he pay the same wth: costs &c.
- ANDREW BAKER being summoned by the Sherriff to answer the presentment of the Grand Jury against him for not goeing to Church for two moneths together and not appeareing, ordered that he be fined according to Law and that he pay the same wth: costs &c.
- Upon the presentment of the Grand Jury against ANDREW HARRISON for turning out and tending second, the Sherriff being ordered last Court to take the said ANDREW HARRISON into custody till he should give security for his appeareance att this court to answer the said presentment, and he being returned by the Sherriff non est inventus and failing to appeare, upon the motion of DANLL. McCARTY, Councell for our Sovereigne Lady the Queene, ordered that the said ANDREW HARRISON be fined according to Law
- Upon the presentment of the Grand Jury against WILLIAM HILL for fishing on the Sabbath Day & he being returned by the Sherriff non est inventus and not appeareing, ordered that he be fined according to Law & that he pay ye same wth: costs &c.
- ABRAHAM HANNISON being summoned by the Sherriff to this Court to answer the presentment of the Grand Jury against him upon suspition

p.   Richmond County Court 7th of March 1704-1708
47   of his living in fornication with MARTHA NEWDALL, who accordingly did
        appeare and entered into security for his refraineing of the company of the sd.

MARTHA NEWDALL till such time as he should make it appear to this Court that his former Wife is dead in order to marry the said MARTHA

- This day FRANCIS STONE acknowledged himselfe indebted to our Sovereigne Lady the Queene in the full and just summe of one hundred pounds Sterl., current money of England, to be paid to our said Sovereigne Lady the Queene her heires and Successors in case ABRAHAM HANNISON do not refrayne the company of MARTHA NEWDALL untill such time as he shall make it appear by a sufficient testimonial from under the Judge of that County Court in MARYLAND where he formerly lived, or any other sufficient caution that the Wife of the said ABRAHAM is now dead

- ABRAHAM HANNISON being summoned by the Sherriff to answer the presentment of the Grand Jury against him for selling Sider on the Sabbath Day and offering no sufficient proofe to the contrary, ordered that he be fined according to Law and that he pay the same wth: costs &c.

- WILLIAM RICHARDSON being summoned by the Sherriff to answer the presentment of the Grand Jury against him for carrying a Gunn in the Woods on the Sabbath Day, and not appeareing, ordered that he be fined according to Law and that he pay the same wth: costs &c.

- CICELY JORDAN being summoned by the Sherriff to answer the presentment of the Grand Jury against her for suffering severall persons to drink sweare and sing att her House on the Sabbath Day and she appeareing but offering no sufficient proofe to the contrary, ordered that she be fined according to Law and that she pay the same wth: costs &c.

- This day JAMES SHERLOCK confest Judgment to the Church Wardens of Northfarnham Parish for the use of the said Parish five hundred pounds of tobbo., it being the fine of ELIZABETH JONES for committing the sin of fornication and having a bastard Child to be paid wth: costs als exo.

p.   Richmond County Court 7th of March 1704/1705
48   - This day THOMAS DICKENSON acknowledged himselfe indebted to the
         Church Wardens of Northfarnham Parish in the full and just summe of ten thousand pounds of good tobbo. & caske to be paid to the Church Wardens theire Exrs. or Admrs. in case ye said THOMAS do not from time to time and att all times hereafter save harmless & keep indemnifyed the said Church Wardens theire Exrs. or Admrs. of and from the charge and trouble whatsoever that shall or may arise or acrew for or by virtue of a bastard Child borne of the body of ELIZABETH JONES

- The presentment of the Grand Jury against MARY CARTER for having a bastard Child is continued till the next Court

- The Order to returne ye valuation of an acre of land for Capt. JOHN TARPLEY to build a Mill upon is dismist, upon his desire

- The Petition of ABRAHAM MARSHALL against JAMES DOOLING is dismist, the Plt. not appeareing to prosecute

- Ordered that JOHN INGO be paid for ten days attendance according to Act by WILLIAM MARSHALL being by him subpaened as an evidence in the suite between the said ABRAHAM, Plt. and ROBERT REYNOLDS, Defendt. als exo

- This day the Last Will and Testament of Majr. DAVID GWYN being presented to this Court by the Exrx. therein named for proofe, the same was proved by

the Oathes of Capt. THOMAS BEALE and JAMES SHERLOCK, two of the wittnesses thereto and Order for Probate granted thereon

    - Upon the motion of Madm. KATHERINE GWYN, Widdo. and Relict of Majr.
DAVID GWYN, Lieut. colo. GEORGE TAYLER, Capt. JOHN TARPLEY, Capt.
THOMAS BEALE & JAMES SHERLOCK, or any three of them, are requested to
meet att the House of Majr. DAVID GWYN, deced., betweene this and the first
Wednesday in June next then and there to inventory all and singular the Estate of
the said Majr. DAVID GWYN as the same shall be presented to theire view and make
report of theire proceedings therein to the succeeding Court under their hands in
writing. (blank) requested to administer an Oath to ye said Madm. KATHERINE
GWYN, Exrx. of the said deced., for the true delivery of the Estate aforesaid

    - Upon the Petition of JOB HAMMOND, JUNR., Guardian and Tutor to
KATHERINE, MERCY & THOMAS BAYLIS, Children of THOMAS BAYLIS the
Elder, deced., against JAMES SUGGITT setting forth that att a Court the said JOB
by an Order of

p.   Richmond County Court 7th of March 1704/1705
49   the Court of September 1703 was appoynted tutor and Guardian to the afore-
    said minors. Whereupon it was ordered that the said JOB should be possest
with all such Estate as to them belonging and praying that the said JAMES SUG-
GITT (who the Plt. in his Petition saith hath by fraud possest himselfe of all the
Estate the Father of the said minors dyed possest with and refuseth to deliver the
same to the said minors) might be summoned to shew cause why he delivers not to
the said JOB to the use of the said minors all and singular the Estate of theire said
Father, being to the value of three hundred pounds Sterl. or thereabouts. Ordered
that the said JAMES SUGGITT be summoned by the Sherriff of this County or his
Deputy to the next Court to shew cause if any he can why the said JOB HAMMOND,
JUNR. on behalfe of each and every of the aforesaid Children be possest of such part
of theire deced. Father's Estate now in the hands of the said JAMES SUGGITT as to
them and every of them doth belong

    - Nonsuite is granted to JOB HAMMOND against JOSHUA HIGHTOWER
for insufficiencies in the Plt.'s Declaration which is ordered to be paid with costs als
exo

    - The Citation granted to JOHN TARPLEY, JUNR. by his Guardian and
prochein ame, JOHN TARPLEY, against the Estate of CORBIN GRIFFIN, Gent.,
late of MIDDLESEX County, deced., is dismist, this Court being of oppinion (after
heareing the plea insisted upon by the Exrs.) that it was not in theire jurisdiction to
trye the same

    - The action of Trespass brought by WINEFRED GLASCOCK by GEORGE
GLASCOCK her prochein amy against EVE SMITH, Widdo., is dismist, ye sd.
Defendt. being dead

    - The action of Trespass brought by NATHANIELL POPE als BRIDGES of
WESTMORELAND County, late of Richmond County, against HENRY LONG is
dismist, the Plt. not prosecuting

    - The action of Trespass brought by CHRISTOPHER PRIDHAM against
LEWIS RICHARDS of the Parish of Northfarnham & County of Richmond, Planter,
is continued att the Defendt.'s request.

    - In the action of Trespass betweene JOHN WHITE and MARGARET his

Wife, Plts. and JOHN SIMONDS, Defendt., for fifty pounds Sterl., damages by means of the Defendt.'s converting to his owne use ten timber trees belonging to and on a certaine tract of land claymed by the Plts. containing three hundred and fifty acres situate lying and being in the Parish of Farnham in the County of Richmond, to which the Defendt., by DANLL. McCARTY his Attorney, pleads Not Guilty in manner and forme. Whereupon the Court have ordered that the Sherriff of this County or his Deputy do summon

p.   Richmond County Court 7th of March 1704/1705
50   a Jury of the most able and antient freeholders of the Vicinage inhabitants as
        neare as may be to the land in controversie and lyble to no just exception either
by affinity consanguinity or interest to meet upon the land aforesaid on the first Monday in Aprill next if faire, if not on ye first faire day after, who being first sworne before Lieut. Colo. SAMLL. PEACHEY or some other of her Majties. Justices for the said County, are required together with Capt. CHARLES SMITH, Surveyor, to survey and lay out the land of the Plts. according to the most antient and reputed bounds of the Pattent thereof, having regard to all Pattents and evidences produced either by the Plts. or Defendt. and all other Elder Pattents adjoyning and that in case they find the Defendt. a Trespasser to value the damage and make report of theire proceedings therein to the next Court under theire hands in writing
        - The Attachment granted last Court to JAMES PHILLIPS against the Estate of JOHN BROWNE is continued till next Court, returnable.
        - The action brought by Majr. WILLIAM ROBINSON against NEHEMIAH JONES is continued att the Defendt.'s requst till next Court
        - The action brought by SYMON PASCOE against GEORGE HARPER is dismist, the Plt. not prosecuting.
        - The action brought by ROBERT JORDAN against WILLIAM LYNTON is dismist for insufficiencies in the Declaration
        - The Attachment granted last Court to THOMAS WHITE against the Estate of THOMAS DECAS is continued till next Court according to Declaration
        - The Attachment granted last Court to THOMAS WHITE against the Estate of ROBERT PAYNE is continued till next Court according to Declaration
        - The Attachment granted last Court to THOMAS WHITE against the Estate of GARRARD NEWTON is continued till next Court according to Declaration
        - The action brought by THOMAS MACKEY against THOMAS WHITE is dismist, the said Defendt. makeing Oath that he marked the hhd. of tobbo.when he was sued with the Plt.'s marke and that he neither directly or indirectly disposed of nor ordered the same to any other person
        - In the action of Debt betweene THOMAS GLOVER, Plt. and PETER OBLEN, Defendt. an Attachment being granted to ye Plt. last Court agt. ye sd. Defendt.'s Estate and by the Sherriff returned to this Court nulla bona, the said suite is therefore dismist
        - The action brought by SAMLL. BAYLY against DAVID YOUNG is dismist, the Plt. not prosecuting

p.   Richmond County Court 7th of March 1704/1705
51   - The action brought by PATRICK CALLAHAN against THOMAS GLAD-
        MAN is dismist, the Plt. not prosecuting

- In the action of Debt betweene CHARLES SMITH, Plt. and PETER OBLEN Defendt., an Attachmt. being granted to the Plt. against the Defendt.'s Estate last Court & by the Sherriff returned to this Court nulla bona, the sayd suite is therefore dismist

- This day JOSHUA LAWSON confest Judgment to WILLIAM HARWOOD for six hundred pounds of tobbo. convenient in Richmond County, which is ordered to be paid wth: costs of suite als exo

- Nonsuite is granted to ANTH0NY SEALE against JOHN GREENE for the insufficiency in the Plt.'s Declaration which is ordered to be paid wth: costs als exo

- The action brought by AVERY NAYER against GEORGE RADFORD is dismist, the Plt. being dead

- Judgment is granted to JOHN TARPLEY against THOMAS MACKEY for two pounds, seven shillings and eight pence which this Court have ordered to be paid wth: costs als exo

- The action brought by HENRY BRERETON againt ELIZA: LYNCH, Admrx. of STEPHEN LYNCH, deced., is continued till next Court

- The action brought by PHEBE SLAUGHTER against HENRY HAYES is dismist, the Plt. not prosecuting

- The action brought by SEM COX against ROBERT LEGG is continued till next Court

- In an action of Debt betweene SEM COX, Plt. and JAMES PHILLIPS, Defendt., for twelve hundred & eighty pounds of tobbo. due by Bill, the Defendt. being callled and not appeareing, Judgment is threfore granted to the Plt. against the Sherriff for the said summe of twelve hundred and eighty pounds of tobbo. unless the Defendt appeares att the next Court and answers the said acton

- Judgment being this day past against the Sherriff unto SEM COX for the non appeareance of JAMES PHILLIPS att the suit of the said SEM for twelve hundred and eighty pounds of tobbo. & caske, upon the motion of the Sherriff an Attachment is granted to him against the Estate of JAMES PHILLIPS for the summe aforesd. returnable to the next Court for Judgment

- In an action of Case betweene SEM COX, Plt. and JAMES PHILLIPS, Defendt., for thirteene hundred seventy five and halfe pounds of tobbo., the Defendt. being called and not appeareing nor any security returned, Judgment is therefore granted to the Plt. against the Sherriff for the summe aforesd. unless the Defendt. appeares at the next Court and answers the said action

p.   Richmond County Court 7th of March 1704/1705
52   - Judgment being this day past against the Sherriff for thirteene hundred & seventy five pounds of tobbo. unto SEM COX for the non appeareance of JAMES PHILLIPS att the suite of the said SEM, upon the motion of the Sherriff an Attachment is granted unto him against the Estate of JAMES PHILLIPS for the summe aforesd. returnable to the next Court for Judgment

- In an action of Debt betweene JOHN FORSTER, Plt. and GEORGE PHILLIPS, Defendt., for nine hundred pounds of tobbo. in caske, the Defendt. being called & not appeareing nor any security returned, Judgment is therefore granted to the Plt. against the Sherriff for the summe aforesd., unless the Defendt appeares att the next Court and answers the said action

- Judgment being this day past against the Sherriff for nine hundred pounds of

tobbo in caske unto JOHN FORSTER for the non appeareance of GEORGE PHILL-
LIPS att the suite of the said JOHN, Upon the motion of the Sherriff, an Attachment is granted unto him against the Estate of GEORGE PHILLIPS for the summe
aforesd. returnable to the next Court for Judgment

    - The action brought by FRANCIS LYNCH against DANLL. McCARTY,
Admr. of DARBY INGLISHBY, is continued till next Court

    - Imparlance granted in the suite betweene JOHN GOWER, Plt. and DANLL.
McCARTY, Admr. of DARBY ENGLISHBY, deced., Defendt., till next Court

    - In an action of Debt between JOHN WORDEN, Plt. and JAMES STORY
Defendt., for eight hundred pounds of tobbo. due by Accot., the Defendt. being called
and not appeareing nor any security returned, Judgment is therefore granted to the
Plt. against the Sherriff for the sume aforesd. unless the Defendt. appeares att the
next Court and answers the said action

    - Judgment being this day past against the Sherrif for eight hundred pounds of
tobbo. unto JOHN WORDEN for the non appeareance of JAMES STORY att the
suite of the said JOHN. Upon the motion of the Sherriff, Attachmt. is granted to him
against the Estate of JAMES STORY for the summe aforesd. returnable to the next
Court for Judgment

    - Nonsuite is granted to JOHN WORDEN for the non appeareance of JAMES
STORY which is ordered to be paid with costs als exo

    - The action brought by EDWARD JEFFEREYS against JAMES STIGE-
LEER is dismist, the Plt. not prosecuting

    - Nonsuite if granted to JEREMIAH HOOKE for the non appeareance of
EDWARD CLERKE which is ordered to be paid wth: costs of suite als exo

    - Nonsuite is granted to STEPHEN (B--------) for the non appeareance of
DANLL. WHITE which is ordered to be paid wth: costs als exo.

p.   Richmond County Court 7th of March 1704/1705
53   - The action brought by JANE (P--Y) against ANDREW SAULSBERRY is
     dismist, the Plt. not prosecuting

    - The action brought by JOHN BOWEN against STEPHEN BOWEN is
dismist, the Plt. not prosecuting

    - The action brought by DANLL. WHITE against THOMAS RICHARDSON
is dismist, the Plt. not prosecuting

    - The action brought by DAVID WILSON against JOHN DOCKER is dismist,
the Plt. not prosecuting

    - In an action of Debt betweene JOHN INGO, Assignee of JAMES INGO, Plt.
and ZACHARIAH NICHOLLS, Defendt. for two hundred and sixty pounds of tobbo.
due by Bill, the Defendt. being returned by the Sherriff non est inventus, Attachment
is therefore granted to the Plt. agaisnt the Estate of the Defendt. for the summe
aforesd. unless the Defendt. appeares att the next Court and answers ye action returnable to the next Court for Judgment

    - The action brought by DAVID BERWICK against MOSES WEBSTER is
dismist, the Plt. not prosecuting

    - In an action of Debt betweene LAWRENCE PRESCOAT, Plt. and HENRY
JENINGS, Defendt., for seven hundred and fifty pounds of good tobbo. in caske upon
his now dwelling Plantation due by Bill, the Defendt. being called and not appeareing

nor any security returned, Judgment is therefore granted to the Plt. agt. the Sherriff for the summe aforesaid unless the Defendt. appeares att the next Court and answers the said action

    - Judgment being this day past against the Sherriff unto LAWRENCE PRES-COAT for the non appeareance of HENRY JENINGS att the suite of the said LAWRENCE for seven hundred and fifty pounds of tobbo. in caske on his now dwelling Plantation, upon the motion of the Sherriff an Attachment is granted him against the Estate of HENRY JENINGS for the summe aforesaid returnable to the next Court for Judgment

    - The action brought by MAURICE FITZGERALD against MICHAEL CONNELE is dismist, the Plt. not prosecuting

    - The action brought by MICHAEL CONNELE against LAWRENCE FOX is dismist, the Plt. not prosecuting

    - In an action of Debt between JOHN TARPLEY, Assignee of EDWARD COLE, Plt. and HENRY PARRY, Defendt. for five hundred & fifty pounds of tobbo. due by Bill, the Defendt. being called and not appeareing, Judgmt. is therefore granted to the Plt. agt. JOSEPH DEEKE, Security returned for his appeareance for the summe aforesd. unless the Defendt. do appeare att ye next Court and answer ye sd. action.

    - The action brought by JOSEPH DEEKE against RICHARD NIXSON is dismist, the Plt. not prosecuting

    - The action brought by THOMAS YATES against ZACHARIAH NICHOLLS is dismist, the Plt. not prosecuting

p.   <u>Richmond County Court 7th of March 1704-1705</u>

54   - Judgment renewed by Scire Facias to JOHN TARPLEY & DAVID BERWICK, Church Wardens of Northfarnham Parish for the use of the said Parish against ZACHARIAH NICHOLLS for five hundred pounds of tobbo. which the Court have ordered to be aid wth: former and present costs als exo

    - In an action of Case betweene JOHN INGO, Plt. nd WILLIAM DRAPER, Defendt., for five hundred and twelve pounds of tobbo., the Defendt. being called & not appeareing, Judgment is therefore granted to the Plt. against him and ROBERT PALMER, Security returned for his appeareance for the said summe of five hundred and twelve pounds of tobbo. returnable unless the Defendt. appeares att the next Court and answers the said action

    - In an action of Trespass betweene WINIFRED GLASCOCK by GEORGE GLASCOCK her prochein amy, Plt. and ABRAHAM GOAD, Defendt., the Defendt. being called and not appeareing nor any security returned, Judgment is therefore granted to the Plt. agt. the Sherriff for fifty pounds Sterl. damage according to Declartion unless the Defendt. appeares att the next Court and answers the said action

    - The Justices's Attachment brought by JOSEPH DEEKE against ROBERT BANNEWELL is dismist

    - The action brought by THOMAS PHELPS against MORGAN SWYNEY is dismist, the Plt. not prosecuting

    - This day Capt. ALEXANDER DONIPHAN acknowledged a Deed of Gift to STEPHEN BOWEN: wch: is ordered to be recorded

    - The action brought by JOSHUA DAVIS against RICHARD TALIAFERRO is dismist, the Plt. not prosecuting

- The action brought by BENJAMIN DEVERELL against ANDREW HARRISON is dismist, the Plt. not prosecuting

- The action brought by ROBERT LENNIS and SUSANNA his Wife, late SUSANNA LAWRENCE, against JAMES STIGELEER is dismist, the Plts. not prosecuting

- The action brought by WILLIAM ROBINSON against GEORGE ERWIN is dismist, the Plt. not prosecuting

- The action brought by JAMES SPENDERGRASS against WILLIAM SMITH, Shoemaker, is dismist, the Plt. not prosecuting

- In an action of Debt betweene ALEXANDER DONIPHAN, Plt. and JOHN BROWNE, Defendant, for twelve hundred and seventy three pounds of tobbo., the Defendt. being returned by the Sherriff non est inventus and not appeareing, Attachment is therefore granted to the Plt. agt. ye sd. Defendt.'s Estate for the summe aforesaid returnable to the next Court for Judgment

p.   Richmond County Court 7th of March 1704/1705
55   - The action brought by JOHN JONES against ANDREW BAKER is dismist the Plt. not prosecuting

- The action brought by THOMAS DICKENSON against JAMES INGO is dismist, the Plt. not prosecuting

- Especiall Imparlance is granted in the suite betweene JOHN STORY, Plt. and CICELY JORDAN, Defendt., till next Court

- The action brought by JOHN GOWER against WILLIAM SMITH on the Hill is dismist, the Plt. not prosecuting

- The action brought by PETER EVANS, Assignee of JOHN WRIGHT, Smith, against JOSEPH (R--------D) is dismist, the Plt. not prosecuting

- The action brought by HENRY ASTINE against GEORGE RADFORD is dismist, the Plt. not prosecuting

- The action brought by THOMAS SHORT against WILLIAM DICKENSON is dismist, the Plt. not prosecuting

- The Justices's Attachment granted to PETER EVANS against ye Estate of DANLL. BRIGGS is continued till next Court

- The action brought by WILLIAM ROBINSON against GEORGE ERWIN is dismist, the Plt. not prosecuting

- The action brought by WILLIAM ROBINSON against GEORGE ERWIN is dismist, the Plt. not prosecuting

- The action brought by EDWARD JEFFERYS against JAMES PHILLIPS is dismist, the Plt. not prosecuting

- The action brought by JEREMIAH HOOK against GEORGE FORELAND is dismist for insufficiencies in the Plt.'s Declaration

- The action brought by EDWARD GOULDMAN against GEORGE WEEKLY is dismist, the Plt. not prosecuting

- In an action of Case betweene FRANCIS WILLIAMS, Plt. and JAMES STIGELEER, Defendt., for sixteene hundred and sixteene pounds of tobbo., the Defendt. being called and not appeareing, Judgment is therefore granted to the Plt. against the Sherriff for the said summe of sixteene hundred and sixteene pounds of tobbo. unless the Defendt. appeares att the next Court & answers the said action

- The action brought by WILLIAM LAMBERT against SAMLL. CHURCHILL is dismist, the Plt. not prosecuting
- The Justices's Attachment granted to BRYAN PHILLIPS against the Estate of WILLIAM CAMBELL is continued till next Court

p.   <u>Richmond County Court 7th of March 1704/1705</u>
56   - Upon the information of WILLIAM SISSON against HENRY SEGAR for the said HENRY's concealing a Tythable, ordered that the said HENRY be summoned to the next Court to answer the said information and shew cause if any he can why the said WILLIAM SISSON should not have Judgment against him according to Law
- Ordered that the Sherriff of this County or his Deputy betweene this and the next Court do summon a competent number of men duely qualified for a Grand Jury to make theire appeareance att the sd. next Court & to be then and there sworne a Grand Jury for this County
- Ordered that the Sherriff of this County or his Deputy do summon all the Militia Officers of this County to make theire appeareance att the next Court, there to take the Oath of Allegiance and Supremacy & also Oath of Abjuration
- Judgment upon Attachment is granted to JOHN HARPER against the Estate of WILLIAM CAMBELL for seven hundred and thirty seven pounds of tobbo. attached out of the Estate of the Defendt., which is ordered to be paid wth: costs of suite als exo
- Judgment being this day past against the Sherriff unto WINIFRED GLAS-COCK by GEORGE GLASCOCK her prochein amy for the non appeareance of ABRAHAM GOAD att the suite of the said WINIFRED for fifty pounds Sterl., damage, upon the motion of the Sherriff Attachment is granted him against the Estate of ABRAHAM GOAD for the summe aforesd. returnable to the next Court for Judgmt.
- The Court adjourned till the first Wednesday in May next

- Att a Court held for Richmond County the Second day of May 1705
Present

Lieut. Colo. GEORGE TAYLER   Capt. JOHN TARPLEY
Capt. ALEXANDER DONIPHAN   Capt. THOMAS BEALE,   Justices

- MARKE RYMER, one of the Grand Jury for this County, faileing to appeare with the rest of the Grand Jury to give in theire presentments, ordered that for his contempt he be fined according to Law

p.   <u>Richmond County Court 2nd of May 1705</u>
57   - This day, Capt. CHARLES BARBER, Atto. for and on the behalfe of JOHN CHAPMAN and JANE his Wife, acknowledged a Deed for Land to JOHN CHAPROONE wch: is ordered to be recorded
- This day the Lre. of Attorney made by JOHN CHAPMAN and JANE his Wife to Capt. CHARLES BARBER was proved by the Oath of HENRY JENNINGS and ordered to be recorded
- This day JOHN WHITE and MARGARETT his Wife acknowledged a Deed for Land wth: Bond to the Vestry of the Parish of Northfarnham for the use of the

said Parish wch: is ordered to be recorded and the said MARGARETT being privately examined by the Judges of this Court, declared that shee did freely and voluntarily wth:out any manner of compulsion thereto acknowledge her right of Inheritance to the said Land, which is ordered to be recorded, And the said MARGARETT for an in consideration of her acknowledgment thereof a Ring of twenty shillings value

    - ANNE JONES, Daughter of MARGT. JONES, being presented to this Court by ANNE FENNER, Daughter of JOHN FENNER, and it appeareing that the said ANNE JONES was likely to become a Parish charge, ordered that the said ANNE do serve the said JOHN FENNER andFRANCES his Wife for the terme of eleven yeares from this day, he finding her sufficient apparrell lodging and dyett dureing the said terme

    - Mr. WM. DAN entered Atto. for JOHN CHAPROONE against THOMAS THORNE

    - Ordered that JOHN HARRIS do serve as Constable in the precincts betweene TOTUSKEY & FARNHAM CREEKs for this ensueing yeare in the roome and stead of THOMAS WHITE, and that he repaire to the nearest Magistrate to take the Oath of a Constable

    - Ordered that CHRISTOPHER EDRINGTON do serve as a Constable in the precincts between FOXHALL's MILL and PAPETICK CREEKE · for the ensueing yeare in the roome and stead of JOSEPH AMOND and that he repaire to the nearest Magistrate to take the Oath of a Constable

    - Ordered that JOHN FOSSAKER do serve as a Constable in the roome and stead of WILLIAM ROWLEY for the ensueing yeare from the DOEG SWAMP upwards, and that he repaire to the nearest Magistrate to take the Oath of a Constable

    - Ordered that EDMOND OVERTON do serve in the Office of Constable in the roome and stead of CORNELIUS HARKIN for the ensueing yeare in the precincts betweene MORATICO & FARNHAM CREEKEs, and that he repaire to the nearest Magistrate to take the Oath of a Constable   .

p.   <u>Richmond County Court 2nd of May 1705</u>
58   - Upon the Petition of TIMOTHY ICK·, Servant to JAMES SCOTT, for his Freedome, it being ordered last Court that if the said JAMES did not appeare att this Court, the said TIMOTHY should be acquitted from the service of the sd. JAMES, but the said JAMES not being summoned pursuant to the sd, order, it is therefore ordered that the said Petition be continued and that MARY SCOTT and the said JAMES be summoned to the next Court to shew cause if any they can why the said TIMOTHY should not be discharged from the service of the said JAMES and MARY

    - The Probate of the Last Will & Testament of JAMES SAMFORD continued till next Court

    - Upon the Petition of REBBECKAH OWEN, ordered that EVAN OWEN, Son of the said REBECAH, by reason of his inability to labour be exempted from the payment of levys till such time as it shall please God to restore him the use of his limbs and render him capable thereof

    - This day JAMES STORY acknowledged a Deed for Land to RICHARD CHICHESTER, Esqr., wch: is ordered to be recorded

    - This day JAMES STORY acknowledged the Assignment of the Pattent of the aforesaid Land to RICHARD CHICHESTER, Esqr., wch: is ordered to be recorded

- WILLIAM WOODBRIDGE, Atto. of MARGT. STORY, relinquished her Right of Dower to the said land wch: is ordered to be recorded

- This day JOHN BROWNE confest Judgment to ALEXANDER DONIPHAN for seven hundred and seventy nine pounds of tobbo. wch: is ordered to be paid with costs of suit als exo

- Upon the presentment of the Grand Jury against ABRAHAM HANNASON and MARTHA NEWDALL for fornication, the said ABRAHAM pursuant to the last Court's Order produceing Certificate from Mr. PHILLIP BRISCOE of CHARLES County in the Province of MARYLAND that the Wife of the said ABRAHAM is now dead, the said presentment is therefore dismist and it is ordered that the said ABRA-HAM do not refrayne the company of the said MARTHA or intermarry with her, that the Sherriff of this County or his Deputy do take him into custody till he shall give security for the same according to Law

- This day the Inventory and Appraisment of the Estate of WILLIAM HANKS being presented to this Court by the Admr. of the said deced., the same is ordered to be recorded

- Upon the Petition of SARAH HANKS, ordered that ROWLAND LAWSON, WILLIAM SMOOTE, DOMINICK BENNEHAN & THOMAS BRYANT or any three

p.   Richmond County Court 2nd of May 1705
59   of them do meet att the House of WILLIAM HANKS, deced., and do the Eighth day of this Instant if faire, if not on the next faire day after, and do then and there according to the best of theire Judgmt., divide the Estate of the sd. WIL-LIAM HANKS according to the Inventory and Appraisment thereof by them returned and make Report of theire proceedings therein to the next Court under theire hands in writing

- The presentment of the Grand Jury against WILLIAM CAMBELL is dismist

- Judgment is granted to JAMES PHILLIPS against JOHN BROWNE for two hundred pounds of tobbo. wch: is ordered to be paid wth: costs of suite als exo

- The action brought by Majr. WILLIAM ROBINSON against NEHEMIAH JONES is continued till next Court

- The Attachment continued last Court against the Estate of THOMAS DEACUS att the suite of THOMAS WHITE continued till next Court

- The Attachment continued last Court agt. the Estate of ROBERT PAYNE att the suite of THOMAS WHITE is continued till next Court

- The Attachment continued last Court against the Estate of GERRARD NEWTON att the suite of THOMAS WHITE is dismist, the Defendt. being dead

- The action brought by HENRY BRERETON against ELIZA: LYNCH, Admrx. of STEPHEN LYNCH, is continued till next Court

- This day the Grand Jury of this County appeareing and making returne of theire severall presentments, it is thereupon ordered that the severall persons by them presented be summoned and that the Sherriff of this County or his Deputy do take sufficient security for theire appeareance at the next Court to answer the said presentments, and it is further ordered that the said Grand Jury be dismist & acquitted for this time from theire service in the aforesaid Office

- Ordered by the Court that the Clerk of this County do present to the Justices of this Court a true and perfect Accot. of all the Fines that hath been imposed on any

person within this County since May 1702 att the next laying of the Levye
    - ROBERT HOPKINS haveing made Oath in Court that neither he nor any person to his knowledge hath taken up the Land due to him for the importation of MATHEW EDWARDS & ELIZA. NORWOOD into this Country, Certificate is thereupon granted unto him for one hundred acres of Land as is usual in such cases the right of wch: he assignes in Court to Capt. CHARLES SMITH

p.   Richmond County Court 2nd of May 1705
60   - FRANCIS JAMES haveing made Oath in Court that neither he nor any person to his knowledge had taken up Land due unto him for the importation of THOMAS SMITH into this Country, Certificate is thereupon granted unto him for fifty acres of land as is usual in such cases, the right of which in Court he assignes to Capt. CHARLES SMITH
    - WILLIAM YATES haveing made Oath in Court that neither he nor any person to his knowledge had taken up the Land due unto him for the importation of WILLIAM McDONNELL and JOANE CARE into this Country, Certificate is thereupon granted unto him for one hundred acres of land as is usual in such cases, the right of which he assignes in Court to Capt. CHARLES SMITH
    - CHARLES DODSON, JUNR. haveing made Oath in Court that he nor any person to his knowledge had taken up the Land due unto him for the importation of CHARLES NEELE, JAMES BOILE & JANE SALSBURY into this Country, Certificate is thereupon granted unto him for one hundred and fifty acres of Land as is usuall in such cases, the right of which he assignes to Capt. CHARLES SMITH
    - This Court takeing into consideration the great inconveniences of not haveing the Laws and Statutes and other necessary Law Books wch: would lend much to theire satisfaction in severall cases and Capt. JOHN TARPLEY offerring to send to England for them, it is thereupon thought fitt and accordingly ordered that he send for such Statutes and Law Books as are required to be provided by the Court of each County according to Act of Assembly and that he be paid for the same att the next laying of the Levye
    - The Court takeing into consideration the disorderly behaviour of the people crowding upon the Lawyers att the barr when they are pleading theire Clients's causes, have for regulation thereof ordered that THOMAS BRADLEY do forthwith make a small barr att the end of the barr that is now wth: bannisters to separate it from the Justices's Bench and that he likewise sett up a Bench in it and make a small table of the same dimensions of that in the Courthouse, two formes of eight feet long and two Benches to be sett up in the Jury Roome and that he receive for the same att the laying of the Levy the summe of five hundred and fifty pounds of tobbo.
    - Upon the Petition of Madm. KATHERINE GWYN, for Admon. on the Estte of PATRICK LAUGHEE, deced., HENRY PARKER appeareing and signifying to this Court that he had right of Admon. for the said Estate, and they haveing heard the severall arguments by them presented, the Court are of Judgmt.

p.   Richmond County Court 2nd of May 1705
61   the disposition of the said Estate lyeth wholly in them and that neither the said KATHERINE nor HENRY have right to Admon. by theire Petitions, And upon the motion of the said KATHERINE GWYN do grant her the Admon. of all and singular the Estate of PATRICK LAUGHEE, deced, she giveing security according

to Law.

From which Judgmt. the said HENRY PARKER appeales to the sixth day of the next Genll. Court for a reheareing

- Ordered that Mr. HENRY ASTINE, Mr. JOSEPH BELFIELD, Mr. GEORGE HOPKINS and THOMAS DICKENSON or any three of them do meet att the House of Madam KATHERINE GWYN some time betweene this and the next Court and do then and there inventory and appraise all and singular the Estate of PATRICK LAUGHEE, deced, as the same shall be presented to theire view and make report of theire proceedings therein to the next Court under their hands in writing; Colo. GEORGE TAYLER is requested to administer an Oath to the Appraisers for theire true appraisment of ye said deced.'s Estate as also to the Admrx. for the true delivery thereof

- This day JOHN POUND and JAMES INGO acknowledged themselves indebted to Madam KATHERINE GWYN in the summe of one hundred pounds Sterl. to be paid to the said KATHERINE GWYN in case HENRY PARKER do not prosecute an appeale by him made from an Order of this Court obtained by her for the Admon. of all and singular the Estate of PATRICK LAUGHEE, deced.

- Ordered that JAMES BIDDLECOMB be summoned by the Sherriff to the next Court to answer the presentment of the Grand Jury against him for entertaineing ZACHARIAH NICHOLLS and a woman commonly called MARY MYLADY who are generally suspected to live in adultery together

- Orderd that ZACHARIAH NICHOLLS and the woman comonly called MARY MYLADY be summoned by the Sherriff to the next Court to answer the presentment of the Grant Jury against them upon genll. suspition of theire living in adultery together

- Ordered that EDWARD BARROW be summoned by the Sherriff to the next Court to answer the presentment of the Grand Jury against him for suffering unlawfull toll to be taken att his Mill and not keeping measures and toll dishes according to Law

- Ordered that MARGARETT, late Servant to JOSEPH BELFIELD, now being att JOHN FENNER's, be summoned by the Sherriff to the next Court to answer the presentment of the Grand

p.   Richmond County Court 2nd of May 1705
62   Jury against her for bareing a Molatto bastard

- Ordered that JAMES LINSEY of Sittenburne Parish be summoned by the Sherriff to the next Court to answer the presentment of the Grand Jury agt. him for not goeing to Church for two moneths together

- Ordered that JAMES WILSON of the Parish of Farnham be summoned by the Sherriff to the next Court to answer the presentment of the Grand Jury against him for concealeing a Tythable

- Ordered that EDWARD JEFFERYS, Ordinary Keeper, be summoned by the Sherriff to the next Court to answer the presentment of the Grand Jury against him for sweareing three Oaths

- Ordered that EDWARD JEFFERYS be summoned by the Sherriff to the next Court to answer the presentment of the Grand Jury against him for not selling drink in lawfull measures

- Ordered that JAMES STEVENSON of Farnham Parish be summoned by the Sherriff to answer the presentment of the Grand Jury against him for not goeing to Church for halfe a yeare together

- Ordered that CHRISTOPHER JONES of Sittenburne Parish be summoned by the Sherriff to the next Court to answer the presentment of the Grand Jury against him for carrying a Fishing Nett on the Sabbath Day.

- The Court adjourned till tomorrow eight of the Clock

- Att a Court held for Richmond County the Third day of May 1705

Present

Lieut. colo. GEORGE TAYLER   Capt. JOHN TARPLEY
Capt. ALEXANDER DONIPHAN   Capt. THOMAS BEALE,   Justices

- This day, GARRARD LYNCH, THOMAS RENNELLS and JAMES INGO acknowledged a Bond for Tuition of SAMLL. INGO to FRANCIS LYNCH and DANLL. McCARTY wch: is ordered to be recorded

p.   Richmond County Court 3d of May 1705
63   - This day FRANCIS LUCAS acknowledged a Deed for Land to SAMLL.
          SAMFORD, wch: is ordered to be recorded

- JOB HAMMOND, Atto. for and on behalfe of the said SAMLL. SAMFORD received the acknowledgment of the said Land

- JAMES SUGGITT, Attorney for and on behalfe of ANNE LUCAS, relinquished her Right of Dower to the said Land

- This day Capt. ALEXANDER DONIPHAN acknowledged an Assignment for the one halfe of a certaine parcell or tract of land mentioned in a Conveyance made by GEORGE JONES, deced., to him, to ALEXANDER DONIPHAN, JUNR., wch: is ordered to be recorded

- This day ALEXANDER DONIPHAN, JUNR. acknowledged an Assignment of the one halfe of a certaine tract or parcell of land mentioned in a certaine conveyance made to ALEXANDER DONIPHAN, JUNR. by GEORGE JONES, deced., to JOHN KELLY, which is ordered to be recorded

- Ordered that the Sherriff of this County or his Deputy betweene this & the next Court do summon a competent number of men duely qualifyed for a Grand Jury to make theire appeareance att the said next Court and to be then and there sworne as a Grand Jury for this County

- Ordered that RICHARD TUTT do serve as Surveyor of the Highwayes from PAPETICK CREEK to FOXHALLS's MILL for this ensueing yeare

- Ordered that Mr. GEORGE PAYNE be Surveyor of the Highwayes from GRAVELLY RUNN to STONY HILL for this ensueing yeare

- This day JOHN JENINGS in open Court made choice of ALEXANDER HINSON for his Guardian and it is ordered that FRANCIS WILLIAMS do forthwth: deliver unto him tht part of his deced.'s Father's Estate or is now in his hands and custody and that the said ALEXANDER HINSON give security for the same according to Law

- Upon the motion of ALEXANDER HINSON, ordered that he do take into his care and tuition MARGARETT JENINGS, Daughter of JOHN JENINGS, and that FRANCIS WILLIAMS do deliver unto the said ALEXANDER

p.   <u>Richmond County Court 3d of May 1705</u>
64   the Estate of the said ANNE now in his hands and custody, and that the said
ALEXANDER do give security for the same according to Law
  - The Court adjourned till the first Wednesday in June next

  - At a Court held for Richmond County the Sixth day of June 1705
Present her Majties. Justices

Lieut. Colo. GEORGE TAYLER   Capt. THOMAS BEALE
Lieut. Colo. SAMLL. PEACHEY   Mr. JOSHUA DAVIS   Justices

  - This day Capt. JOHN TARPLEY produceing to this Court his Excellencies
Commission for him to be Sherriff of this County wch: being openly read and he
haveing taken the Oaths appointed by Act of Parliament to be taken instead of the
Oaths of Allegiance and Supremacy and subscribed the Test, was accordingly
sworne SHERRIFF of the said County
  - This day JOHN DOYLE haveing taken the Oaths appointed by Act of Par-
liament to be taken instead of the Oaths of Allegiance and Supremacy and subscri-
bed the Test was also sworne UNDER SHERRIFF of this County
  - This day the Inventory of the Estate of Majr. DAVID GWYN, being pre-
sented to this Court by Lieut. Colo. GEORGE TAYLER, one of the Gent. appointed to
inventory the said Estate, the same is ordered to be recorded
  - This day the Inventory and Appraisment of the Estate of PATRICK
LAUGHEE, being presented to this Court by Mr. HENRY ASTINE, one of the
Appraisers of the said Estate, the same is ordered to be recorded
  - This day the Lre. of Attorney made by THOMAS SMALLWOOD & RALPH
(P------) of Liverpoole to Capt. JOHN GREENE was proved by the Oath of ROBERT
MASON and ordered to be recorded
  - This day the Lre. of Attorney made by JANE PAICE to DANLL. WHITE
was proved by the Oaths of GEORGE PAYNE & TIMOTHY ICK & ordered to be
recorded

p.   <u>Richmond County Court 6th of June 1705</u>
65   - This day the Letter of Attorney made by JOHN LLOYD, Esqr. to GRIFFIN
FAUNTLEROY was proved by the Oaths of LAWRENCE CLIFTON and
GEORGE BRERETON and ordered to be recorded
  - Betty, an Indian Girl belonging to JOB HAMMOND, being by him presented
to this Court to have inspection into her age is adjudged six yeares old
  - Upon the Complaint of Colo. WILLIAM TAYLOE setting forth tht in pursuance of his Excellencies Proclamation and also of one Order of his Excellency in
Councell of the 21th of 8br. 1704, and of a further Order from his Excellency to him
directed for the speedy apprehending and secureing of all goods and chattels belonging
to the NANSATICO INDIANS, in order for the removeing thereof to the Citty of
WILLIAMSBURGH, to be safely delivered to his Excellency for her Majties's use, he
the said Colo. WM. TAYLOE on the 23d day of May last past issued his speciall warrant directed to the Sherriff of Richmond County or his Deputy to make diligent Enquiry and search of the goods and chattels of the INDIANS aforesaid; in obedience to
wch: preceipt, GARRARD LYNCH, Under Sherriff of this County, on the 24th day of
May last came before him and made Complt. that in pursuance of the aforesd. pre-

cept from him directed to the Sherriff or his Deputy for the searching and apprehending of goods and chattels aforesd., he went to the House of WILLIAM STONE for a kettle being the goods of the aforesd. INDIANS and wch: the said STONE had then in his custody and required the same of the said STONE and that he should carry him where the rest of the goods att that time were, and that the said STONE refused to obey the Sherriff and that the said STONE wth: opprobrious and abusive words reviled his Excellency and him, the said Collo. WM. TAYLOE, saying that if his Excellency and the said Coll. WM. TAYLOE had been there he would not have obeyed them. Upon consideration of the whole matter according to the Complt. of the said Coll. WILLIAM TAYLOE for the Contempt offered by him the said WILLIAM STONE and upon the prayer of the said Coll. WILLIAM TAYLOE, the Court have ordered that the Sherriff of this County or his Deputy do forthwth; take into his custody the body of the said WILLIAM STONE and him in his safe custody to keep till he shall enter into Bond wth: security for Five hundred pounds Sterl., for his appearance att the next Court to answer the Contempt aforesd.

    - Upon the Complt. of Lieut. Colo. SAMLL. PEACHEY against LAWRENCE FOX for his Contempt in refuseing & forcibly withstanding of RICHARD HOLLISTER and THOMAS LLOYD (impowered by a Warrant in her Majties behalfe issued by the said SAMLL. PEACHEY to them directed) to make search in his house

p.   Richmond County Court 6th of June 1705
66   upon suspicion of his stealeing a Lamb belonging to him, the said SAMLL. PEACHEY. Ordered that the Sherriff of this County or his Deputy do take into his custody the body of the said LAWRENCE FOX and him in safe custody to keep until he give Bond with sufficient security for his appeareacne att the next Court to answer the said Contempt

    - This day JOHN JENNINGS made choice in open Court of GEORGE ERWIN for his Guardian and it is ordered that FRANCIS WILLIAMS do deliver unto the said GEORGE for the use of the said JOHN JENNINGS all the Estate belonging to the said JOHN now in his hands & custody, the said GEORGE ERWIN giving security for the same according to Law, and it is likewise ordered that the said GEORGE ERWIN do instruct the sd. JOHN JENNINGS in his reading

    - This day WILLIAM SIMMS and JAMES INGO acknowledged themselves indebted unto the Worspll. her Majties. Justices for Richmond County in the full & just summe of twenty thousand pounds of tobbo. to be paid to the sd. Justices their heires Exrs. and Admrs. in case GEORGE ERWIN, Guardian & Tutor of JOHN JENNINGS do not surrender unto the said Justices or such person as shall be by them appointed to received the same for the use of the said JOHN JENNINGS all and singular the Estate of the said JOHN and render a true Accot. thereof when thereunto lawfully required

    - Ordered that Capt. WILLIAM UNDERWOOD and Capt. ALEXANDER DONIPHAN do take the List of Tythables this present yeare in theire respective precincts as formerly

    - Ordered that the Sherriff of this County or his Deputy do summon a competent number of men duely qualified for a Grand Jury to make theire appeareance att the sd. next Court and to be then & there sworne a Grand Jury for this County

    - MICHAELL OWEN, Servant to JOHN COOMBS, being presented to this Court for inspection into his age is adjudged thirteene yeares old and ordered that he

Levy free till the age appoynted for paymt. of a Levy

    - Upon the Petition of TIMOTHY ICK for his Freedome, JAMES SCOTT, the said TIMOTHY's present Master and MARY SCOTT being by last Court's Order summoned to appeare att this Court to answer to the said Petition and shew cause if any they could why the said TIMOTHY should not be free, the said JAMES and MARY fayling to appeare according to the said Order, and it evidently appeareing

p.   <u>Richmond County Court 6th of June 1705</u>
67   by the Oaths of ELINOR FORSTER, JOYCE FLETCHER and WILLIAM ICK that the said TIMOTHY had but foure yeares to serve by Indenture and that the sd. ELINOR FORSTER did read his Indenture, she being bound att the same time, it is therefore ordered that the said TIMOTHY ICK be free and that the said JAMES SCOTT do pay him his Corne and Cloathes according to Act wth: costs als exo

    - Ordered that ELINOR FORSTER be paid by TIMOTHY ICK for two days attendance according to Act being by him subpaened as an evidence betweene the said TIMOTHY, Plt. and JAMES SCOTT, Defendt., als exo

    - Ordered that WILLIAM ICK be paid by TIMOTHY ICK for two days attendance according to Act being by him subpaened as an evidence in the difference betweene the said TIMOTHY, Plt. and JAMES SCOTT, Defendt., als exo

    - AVERY DYE by his nearest Friend and Father, ARTHUR DYE, exhibiting his Bill in Chancery against PATIENCE NAYLER, Exrx. of the Last Will and Testament of AVERY NAYLER, deced., ordered that her Majties. most gratious Writt of Subpaena do issue directed to the said PATIENCE in her qualification aforesd. requiring her to appeare att the next Court and answer the said Bill

    - Upon the motion of Mr. WILLIAM DAVIS, ordered that the Letter from NEHEMIAH JONES directed to him be recorded

    - Upon the Petition of JOHN MOLTON, ordered that ROBERT PORT do forthwth: keepe and cleane the Rowling Way from his tobbo. house which has alwayes beene reputed and knowne for a common Rowling House

    - The Court is adjourned till the first Wednesday in July next

    - Att the Courthouse of Richmond County, August the First 1705

    - This day FRANCIS SLAUGHTER acknowledged a Deed for Land to WILLM. MARSHALL in the presence of Colo. GEORGE TAYLER & Capt. ALEXR. DONIPHAN; and EDWARD TURBERVILE, Attorney of MARGT. SLAUGHTER, relinquished her Right of Dower to the said Land all wch: was by them ordered to be recorded

    - This day, EDWARD TURBERVILE, Atto. of KATHERINE DAVIS, relinquished her Right of Dower of three hundred and fifteene acres of Land sold by her Husband, Mr. JOSHUA DAVIS, to Capt. ALEXR. DONIPHAN in presence of Colo. GEORGE TAYLER and ye said Capt. DONIPHAN wch: is by them ordered to be recorded

p.
68

- Att a Court held for Richmond County the 5th day of September 1705
Present

Lieut. Colo. GEORGE TAYLER	Capt. THOMAS BEALE
Lieut. Colo. SAMLL. PEACHEY	Capt. CHARLES BARBER
Capt. ALEXR. DONIPHAN	Mr. JOSHUA DAVIS Justices

- This day his Excellency's Proclamation for continueing all Officers in theire respective places and for dissolving the present Assembly & also one other Proclamation for the Election of Burgesses was by Order of this Court openly read & published

- This day the Last Will and Testament of DANLL. HORNEBY being presented to this Court by Mr. THOMAS SUGGITT, one of the Trustees in the said Will named, for proofe, the same was proved by the Oaths of THOMAS BARLOW and HENRY JENINGS and Order for Probate granted thereon

- Ordered that Capt. HENRY BRERETON, Mr. GYLES WEBB, Mr. JAMES SUGGITT & Mr. EDGCOMB SUGGITT or any three of them sometime betweene this and the next Court do meet att the House of Mr. JOHN TAVERNER and do then and there inventory all and singular the Estate of DANLL. HORNEBY, deced., as the same shall be presented to theire view and make report of theire proceedings therein to ye said next Court under their hands in writing

- This day ANTHONY CARNABY acknowledged a Deed for Land to WILLIAM PILKINTON, wch: is ordered to be recorded. ELIZA: CARNABY, Wife of the said ANTHONY, relinquished her Right of Dower to the said Land

- This day JOB HAMMOND	JOB HAMMOND, JUNR.	GILBERT CROSSWELL
PHILLIP HARRIS	NATHLL. THRIFT	THOMAS JESPER
WM. ALGOOD	GABRIELL ALLOWAY	WILLIAM LAMBERT
WM. MISKELL	WM. SMITH, Tanner	CHARLES CALE,
CHARLES STEWARD	STEPHEN HOWELL	JOHN WILLIS, JUNR.
GEORGE GREENE	WILLIAM WILLIS	WILLIAM TRIPLETT
FRANCIS WILLIAMS	JOHN BROWNE	MARTIN FISHER
JOHN BERRY	GEORGE HOPKINS and	WILLIAM PITTMAN

being summoned to serve as a Grand Jury for this County did accordingly appeare and were sworne

- This day GEORGE GLASCOCK acknowledged a Deed for Land to HENRY CLARKE wch: is ordered to be recorded

- Mr. DANIELL McCARTY according to his power from MILLION GLASCOCK, Wife of the said GEORGE GLASCOCK, relinquished her Right of Dower to the said Land

- This day the Lre. of Attorney made by JOHN INGO to JAMES INGO was proved by the Oaths of WILLIAM (   ) and DOROTHY DURHAM and ordered to be recorded

- This day, DANLL. McCARTY by virtue of a Power of Attorney to him from SAMLL. BAYLY acknowledged a Deed for Land to WILLIAM BARBER & JOYCE his Wife which is ordered to be recorded

p.
69

Richmond County Court 5th of September 1705

- The Lre. of Attorney made by SAMLL. BAYLY to DANLL. McCARTY was this day proved by the Oath of Capt. CHARLES BARBER

- This day WILLIAM BARBER and JOYCE his Wife acknowledged a Deed for

Land to Capt. CHARLES BARBER wch: is ordered to be recorded; And the said
JOYCE being privately examined did voluntarily confess and acknowledge tht she did
the same wth:out any manner of compulsion thereto wch: is likewise ordered to be
recorded

    - This day JAMES INGO acknowledged a Deed for Land with Bond to THO-
MAS DURHAM wch: is ordered to be recorded and the said JAMES INGO, Atto. for
and on the behalfe of JOHN INGO, acknowledged the said JOHN INGO's Title to the
sd Land which is also ordered to be recorded

    - This day the Lre. of Attorney made by Mr. HENRY ASTINE to his Wife,
ANNE ASTINE and SAMLL. GODWIN was proved by the Oaths of THOMAS
WARD and RICHARD THODY and ordered to be recorded

    - This day JAMES INGO acknowledged a Deed for Land with Bond to RAW-
LEIGH DOWNEMAN which is ordered to be recorded

    - Ordered that Capt. JNO. TARPLEY do take into his Custody one Negro man
taken up in tis County by JNO. YEATMAN, who is required to notify the same att all
publick places and to keep the said Negro till his Master or some other persons do
appeare wth: a sufficient power from him to remand the said Negro out of the hands
of the said Capt. JNO: TARPLEY

    - It evidently appeareing to this Court that RICHARD DONELEY, Servant to
Doctor ROBERT CLARKE had absented himselfe by running away att severall
times out of the service of his said Master the space of fifty foure days and that he
had expended in procureing him againe att the severall times of his absence the
summe of eight hundred and fifty pounds of tobbacco. Ordered that he serve his said
Master or his assignes the terme of fourteene moneths after his tme by Indenture
Custome or otherwise be fully expired

    - Upon the Petition of HUGH FRENCH, one of the Sons of HUGH FRENCH,
late of this County, deceased, by WILLIAM TRIPLETT his prochein amy, setting
forth that his Father, HUGH FRENCH, deced., did by his Last Will and Testament
inter alia give and devise to each of his Sons a feather bed furniture sheets a horse
and five thousand pounds of tobbo.. to be paid to each of them when they should
attaine to ye age of sixteene & to each of them a pott and frying pann and made his
then Wife, MARGT., Exrx. of his said Will & yt. ye said MARGRETT hath since the
death of the aforesd. Testator proved the sd. Will and accepted the Executrixship and
is since intermarryed wth: one JNO. SOMMERVILL & that the said MARGT. while
sole or the aforesd. JOHN and MARGARETT since theire being marryed, the aforesd.
feather bed furniture sheets horse five thousand pounds of tobbo. pott and frying
pann or any part or parcell thereof to him the aforesd. HUGH (he being long since
arrived to the age of sixteene yeares) to deliver and pay altho often required have and
still

p.   <u>Richmond County Court 5th of September 1705</u>
70   doe refuse and deny, but the same & every part & parcell thereof doe unjustly
      keep and detaine. It is therefore ordered that the said JOHN & MARGT. Exrx.
as aforesd., be called to appeare att the next Court to shew cause if any they can why
they render and pay not unto the aforesd. HUGH FRENCH his Legacy aforesaid so
due as aforesaid & for wch: by his prochein amy aforesd. he humbly prays Order for
wth: costs

    - It appeareing to this Court by Certificate from Capt. ALEXANDER DONI-

PHAN that WILLIAM BRINN, Servant to Mr. JOSHUA DAVIS, had absented him-selfe from his Master's service the terme of six weeks and that he had expended the summe of six hundred and thirty pounds of tobbo. to procure him againe. Ordered that he serve his said Master or his assignes the space of eight moneths after the time by Indenture Custome or otherwise be fully expired

- Upon the Petiton of MARY JONES agt. FRANCIS WILLIAMS for her Corne and Cloathes according to Act and it appeareing to this Court that she had received some part thereof, Ordered that the said FRANCIS WILLIAMS do pay unto the said MARY two barrells of Indian Corne, one paire of stockins, a woollen petticoat & linen to make her a Cap & that he pay costs

- Upon the Petition of ROBERT PECK, ordered that he be levy free for the future by reason of his age and inability to labour

- GEORGE ERWIN haveing made Oath in Court that neither he nor any per-son to his knowledge have taken up the Land due to him for importation of EDWARD ROARK, SARAH CARNABY & SARAH ERWIN into this Colony, Certificate is thereupon granted him for one hundred and fifty acres of Land as is usuall in such cases the right of wch: he assignes in Court to Capt. CHARLES SMITH

- WILLIAM STROTHER haveing made Oath in Court that he nor any person to his knowledge have taken up the Land due unto him for the importation of JOHN WISE, ELEXR. DUDLEY, REDMOND PEASLEY, JNO: KNIGHT, WILLIAM TURNER, SARAH IRELAND & WILLIAM CUNNINGHAM into this Colony, Cer-tificate is thereupon granted unto him for three hundred and fifty acres of land as is usuall in such cases, the right of which in Court he assignes to Capt. CHARLES SMITH

- SIMON MILLER haveing made Oath in Court that neither he nor any per-son to his knowledge have taken up the Land due unto him for the importation of MARGARETT BUTTLER and JOHN MORGAN into this Colony, Certificate is thereupon granted unto him for one hundred acres of Land as is usuall in such cases, the right of which in Court he assignes to Capt. CHARLES SMITH

- Capt. WILLIAM BARBER haveing made Oath in Court that neither he nor any persons to his knowledge have taken up the Land due to him for the importation of ROBERT RATELEPH, WILLIAM EDGE, CORNELIUS CARRY, RICHARD BENTLY and ELIZABETH

p.
71   Richmond County Court 5th of September 1705
       (? GARMALS) into this Colony, Certificate is thereupon granted unto him for
       one hundred and fifty acres of Land as is usuall in such cases, the right of
which he assignes unto Capt. CHARLES SMITH

- WILLIAM PANNELL haveing made Oath in Court that neither he nor any persons to his knowledge have taken up the Land due to him for the importation of WILLIAM MARKHAM, MARGRETT LAMB & EDWARD THORNCRAFT into this Colony, Certificate is thereupon granted unto him for one hundred and fifty acres of land as is usuall in such cases the right of wch: in Court he assignes to Capt. CHARLES SMITH

- CHRISTOPHER JONES haveing made Oath in Court that neither he nor any person to his knowledge have taken up the land due to him for the importation WILLIAM EIKE into this Colony, Certificate is thereupon granted him as is usuall in such cases the right of wch: in Court he assignes to Capt. CHARLES SMITH

- MARTIN FISHER haveing made Oath in Court that neither he nor any person to his knowledge have taken up the land due to him for the importation of JOSEPH MINTON & HENRY MINTON into this Colony, Certificate is thereupon granted unto him for one hundred acres of Land as is usuall in such cases, the right of wch; in Court he assignes to Capt. CHARLES SMITH

- This day the Last Will and Testament of THOMAS BRADLEY being presented to this Court for proofe by the Exectr. therein named, the same was proved by the Oaths of JOHN KELLY and WILLIAM SHAW and Order for Probate granted thereon

- This day JOHN WRIGHT acknowledged a Deed for Land with Bond to Mr. FRANCIS THORNTON, wch: is ordered to be recorded

- Majr. FRANCIS WRIGHT, Father of the sd. JOHN WRIGHT, acknowledged his Right and Title that he had to the Land aforesd., wch: is ordered to be recorded

- Majr. FRANCIS WRIGHT acknowledged a Bond for performance of Covenants to Mr. FRANCIS THORNTON, wch: is ordered to be recorded

- WILLIAM THORNTON, Son of the aforesd. FRANCIS THORNTON, received the acknowledgmts. of the Deeds and Bonds aforesd.

- This day JAMES CAWARD haveing taken the Oaths appointed by Act of Parliamt. to be taken instead of the Oaths of Allegiance and Supremacy and subscribed the Test tooke also the Oath of Abjuration and was sworne UNDER SHERRIFF of this County

- The Court is adjourned till the first Wednesday in October next

p.
72
- Att a Court held for Richmond County the 3d day of October 1705
                    Present
Lieut. Colo. GEORGE TAYLER   Capt. ALEXR. DONIPHAN
Lieut. Colo. SAMLL. PEACHEY   Capt. THOMAS BEALE   Justices
Capt. JNO: DEANE   Mr. JOSHUA DAVIS

- This day the Last Will and Testament of CHARLES TEBO, being presented to this Court by the Exrx. therein named for proofe, the same was proved by the Oaths of RICHARD TANKERSLEY and WILLIAM MARSHALL and Order for Probate granted thereon

- This day the Last Will and Testament of THOMAS TILLREY being presented to this Court by the Executr. therein named for proofe, the same was proved by the Oaths of THOMAS JENKIN and JAMES COWARD and Order for Probate granted thereon

- This day, EDWARD GEOFFEREY acknowleged an Assignment of a Patent for Land granted to Mr. HENRY WILSON to THOMAS GEOFFERY, wch: is ordered to be recorded

- Jack, a Negro boy belonging to MRS. PATIENCE NAYLER adjudged eight yeares old

- This day FRANCES TEBO acknowledged a Deed of Guift to her Son, JOHN TEBO, wch: is ordered to be recorded

- Upon the Petition of WILLIAM HANKS that he might be admitted to build a Mill on a certaine Runn or water course in this County called FARNHAM CREEKE and EDWARD GEOFFEREY appeareing and declareing he was willing that he should have the liberty of land as the Law prescribes, ordered that (blank) or any three of them sometime betweene this and the next Court do lay out and value an acre of land on the opposite side of the said Runn and make report of theire proceedings therein to the sd. next Court under theire hands in writing

- This day ROBERT CLARKE acknowledged a Deed of Land to ROBERT CLARKE, JUNR., wch: is ordered to be recorded

- WILLIAM HALL, MORRIS JONES and GEORGE GUY, Servants to Mr. PETER KIPPAX, being by virtue of a Precept from Lieut. Colo. SAMLL. PEACHEY summoned to appeare att this Court and answer to the information of theire said Master against them for theire stealeing and

p.   Richmond County Court 3d of October 1705
73   killing of a Hog belonging to him, the said WILLIAM HALL, MORRIS JONES
        and GEORGE GUY appeareing and severally acknowledging and confessing
that they were Guilty of the aforesaid Crime, it is therefore ordered that the said WM. HALL, MORRIS JONES and GEORGE GUY be severally fined according to the Act of Assembly in that case made & provided, vizt., tht they severally serve the said Mr. PETER KIPPAX the terme of two yeares after their times by Indenture custome or otherwise be expired or otherwise that each of them pay unto theire said Master the summe of two thousand pounds of tobbo. als exo

- JANE RYALL, Servt. to JOHN WILSON, being presented to this Court for committing the sin of fornication and having a bastard Child and the said JANE refuseing to confess who was the Father of her said Child, they have therefore thought fitt to have an (Latin term) for the perusall of the Law in that case made & provided returnable tomorrow morning

- The Court adjourned till tomorrow morning Eight of the Clock

- Att a Court held for Richmond County the 4th day of October 1705
                        Present
Coll. WM. TAYLOE   Mr. ALEXR. DONIPHAN
Lieut. Colo. GEORGE TAYLER   Mr. JOSHUA DAVIS   Justices
Lieut. Colo. SAMLL. PEACHEY

- In the Citation brought by JOB HAMMOND, JUNR. Guardian and Tutor to KATHERINE, MERCY and THOMAS BAYLIS, Children of THOMAS BAYLIS the Elder, deced., against JAMES SUGGITT, the said Defendt. failing to appeare, conditional order is therefore granted to the said JOB in behalfe of the said Orphans for such part of the said Children's Estate in the hands of the said JAMES SUGGITT as to them and every of them do belong unless the said JAMES SUGGITT do appeare att the next Court and shew cause to the contrary

- The action brought by CHRISTOPHER PRIDHAM against LEWIS RICHARDS of the Parish of Northfarnham and County of Richmond, Planter, is dismist, the Plt. not prosecuting

p.   Richmond County Court 4th of October 1705
74   - The action brought by JAMES PHILLIPS against JOHN BROWNE is
        dismist, the Plt. not prosecuting

- The action brought by HENRY BRERETON against ELIZABETH LYNCH, Admrx. of STEPHEN LYNCH, deced., is dismist, the Plt. not prosecuting

- The action brought by SEM COX against ROBERT LEGG is dismist, the Plt. not prosecuting

- The action of Case brought by SEM COX against ROBERT LEGG is dismist, the Plt. not prosecuting

- The action of Debt brought by SEM COX against JAMES PHILLIPS is continued till next Court by consent

- The action of Case brought by SEM COX against JAMES PHILLIPS is continued till next Court by consent

- Upon the Petition of ANNE GREENE, Order for Admon. is granted to her on all and singular the Estate of RICHARD GREENE, she giving security according to Law

- This day Capt. JOHN CRASKE and JNO: POUND acknowledged themselves indebted unto the Worsppll. her Majties Justices for Richmond County in the full and just summe of two hundred pounds Sterl., to be payd to the said Justices theire Exrs. or Admrs. in case ANNE GREENE do not duely administer on all and singular the Estate of RICHARD GREENE, deced., & render a true Account thereof when thereunto lawfully called

- In the action of Debt betweene JOHN FOSSAKER, Plt. and GEORGE PHILLIPS, Defendt. for nine hundred pounds of tobbo. due by Bill, ordered that unless the Defendt. do appeare att the next Court and prove the paymt. of the said tobbo., Judgmt. be confirmed agt. him for the same wth: costs

- Judgment is granted to FRANCIS LYNCH againt DANLL. McCARTY, Admr. of the goods and chattells of DARBY INGLISHBY, deced., for twenty eight pounds, foure shillings and one penny Sterl., due by Accot. proved by the Oath of the Plt., if so much of the Estate of the said deced. remaines in the hands of his Admr. aforesaid to be paid with costs of suite als exo

- The action brought by JOHN GOWER agt. DANLL. McCARTY, Admr. of DARBY INGLISHBY, deced., is dismist, the Plt. not prosecuting

- The Order granted last Court against the Sherriff to JOHN WORDEN for the non appeareance of JAMES STOREY is continued till next Court

- The action brought by JOHN INGO, Assignee of JAMES INGO, against ZACHARIAH NICHOLLS is dismist, the Plt. not prosecuting

- The action brought by LAWRENCE PRESCOAT agt. HENRY JENINGS is dismist, the Plt. not prosecuting

- The action brought by JNO. WHITE and MARGT. his Wife agt. JOHN SIMONS is continued till next Court

p. 75   Richmond County Court 4th of October 1705
- In an action of Debt betweene JOHN TARPLEY, Assignee of EDWARD COLE, Plt. and HENRY PARRY, Defendt. for five hundred and fifty pounds of tobbo. due by Bill, the said Defendt. not appeareing to answer the same, the Judgment of the last Court is therefore confirmed to the Plt. against JOSEPH DEEKE, Security returned for the said Defendt.'s appeareance for the said summe of five hundred and fifty pounds of tobbo. and it is ordered that he pay the same to the Plt. wth: costs als exo.

- In an action of Case betweene JNO: INGO, Plt. and WILLIAM DRAPER, Defendt., for five hundred and twelve pounds of tobbo. due by Accot., the Defendt. not appeareing to answer the same, the Judgment of the last Court is therefore confirmed to the Plt. against ROBERT PALMER, Security returned for the said Defendt.'s appeareance for the sd summe of five hundred & twelve pounds of tobbo. and it is ordered that he pay the same with costs als exo

   - Mr. GEORGE ESKRIDGE entered Attorney for JOHN SOMERVELL

   - In an action of Trespass betweene WINIFRED GLASCOCK by her prochein amy, GEORGE GLASCOCK, Plt. and ABRAHAM GOAD, Defendt., for fifty pounds Sterl., damage by meanes of the Defendt.'s (on or about the tenth day of Janry. last by force and arms and contrary to the peace, &c.) entering upon, falling cutting downe carrying away and converting to his owne use five timber trees belonging to and on the land of the Plt.and also for committing severall other trespasses thereon wch; sd. Land containing two hundred and eighty acres wth: the appurtenances is situate lying and being in the Parish of Northfarnham and County of Richmond;

To which the Defendt. in proper person pleads Not Guilty. Whereupon it is ordred that the Sherriff of this County or his Deputy do summons a Jury of the most able and antient freeholders of the County Inhabitants as neare as may be to the land in controversie and lyable to no just exception for affinity consanguinity or interest to meet on the last Monday in November next if faire if not the next faire day after on the land aforesaid, who being first sworne before Collo. SAMLL. PEACHEY or any other Justices having regard to all evidences offered by Plt. or Defendt. are required to survey and lay out in company with Capt. CHARLES SMITH, Surveyor, the Land of the Plt. according to the most antient & reputed bounds of the Patent thereof, and make report of theire proceedings threin to the next Court under theire hands in writing and if they do find ye Defendt. a Trespasser to value ye damages & report the same

   - This day the Last Will and Testament of EVE SMITH being presented to this Court by ABRAHAM GOAD for proofe, the same was proved by Oaths of CHARLES DODSON & ANNE DODSON, and Order of Probate granted thereon

   - The action brought by ALEXANDER DONIPHAN agt. JNO: BROWNE is dismist, the Plt. not prosecuting

p.   <u>Richmond County Court 4th of October 1705</u>
76   - The action brought by JOHN IKEY agt. CISLEY JORDAN is dismist, the Plt. not prosecuting

   - In the action of Case betweene HENRY ASTINE, Plt. and GEORGE RADFORD, Defendt., for one thousand pounds of tobbo. damage by meanes of the Defendt. takeing beareing away and converting to his owne use one parcell of tobbo. out of a hhd. being in the tobbo. house of him the Plt., amounting to the summe of foure hundred pounds of tobbo. or thereabouts,

To which the said Defendt. in proper person came into Court and pleaded Not Guilty Whereupon a Jury was impannelled and sworne to try the matter in issue by name

ROBERT PAYNE	JOHN SETTLE	JAMES TRENT
JOHN BOWEN	JNO. GRIMSLEY	JOB HAMMOND, JUNR.
ALEXANDER FLEMING	WILLIAM YATES	PETER EVANS
JOHN KELLY	JAMES SUGGITT	JNO: WILLIS, JUNR.

who being returned brought in for Verdict, We of the Jury do find for the Plt. one thousand pounds of tobbo. damage, wch: Verdict upon the motion of GEORGE ESKRIDGE, Attorney for the Plt., is by this Court confirmed and ordered that the said GEORGE RADFORD do pay the same together with costs of suite als exo.

- The Attachment granted last Court to PETER EVANS agt. the Estate of DANLL. BRIGGS is continued till next Court
- In an action of Case betweene FRANCIS WILLIAMS, Plt. and JAMES STIGELEER, Defendt., for fifteene hundred & fifty pounds of tobbo. due to ye Plt. by Order of this Court from the same JAMES or his Security for his appeareance att a Court held for this County att the suite of JAMES PHILLIPS for the summe aforesd. wch: together wth: the cost of suite did amount to the summe of sixteene hundred and sixteene pounds of tobbo., and the said Defendt. being called and not appeareing nor any security returned, it is therefore ordered that the last Court's Order be confirmed against CHARLES BARBER, late Sherriff, and that he pay unto the sd, FRANCIS WILLIAMS the summe of one thousand & ten pounds of tobbo. being the ballance of the abovesd. Order, together wth: costs of suite als exo
- The Justices's Attachment brought by BRYAN PHILLIPS against WILLIAM CAMBELL is dismist, neither party appeareing
- The Information exhibited by WILLIAM SISSON agt. HENRY SEGAR is dismist, the Plt. not prosecuting
- The action brought by MARY GILBERT against JNO. INGO is dismist, the Plt. not prosecuting
- In the suite if Chancery commenced by JOHN TARPLEY, JUNR., by JOHN TARPLEY, his Father and prochein amy, against CHRISTOPHER ROBINSON and JUDITH

p.   <u>Richmond County Court 4th of October 1705</u>
77   his Wife & THOMAS GRIFFIN and PETER PRESSLEY and WINIFRED his Wife, Exrx. of the Last Will and Testament of CORBIN GRIFFIN, deced., for thirty pounds Sterl. due to the said JNO. TARPLEY, JUNR. as a Legacy given him by the said deced., and the said Defendts. being called and not appeareing nor any security returned, upon the motion of the Plt., an Attachment is granted him against the Estate of the said deced., in the hands of his Exors. aforesaid for the said sume of thirty pounds Serl. returnable to the next Court for Judgment
- The action brought by JAMES CAWARD against ROBERT FRISTOE is dismist, the Plt. not prosecuting
- The action brought by JAMES GIBBIN against ALEXANDER CAMBELL is dismist, the Plt. not prosecuting
- The action brought by THOMAS PEARCE against ZACHARIAH NICHOLLS is dismist, the Plt. not prosecuting
- The action brought by JNO: WHITE against CHARLES DODSON, JUNIOR is dismist, the Plt. not prosecuting
- The action brought by JNO: WHITE against CHARLES DODSON, JUNR. is dismist, the Plt. not prosecuting
- The action brought by ROBERT FRISTOE against JAMES CAWARD is dismist, the Plt. not prosecuting
- The action brought by JAMES CAWARD against SAMLL. BAYLY is dismist, the Plt. not prosecuting
- The action brought by JOHN TARPLEY against THOMAS JENKIN is dismist, the Plt. not prosecuting
- The action brought by ALEXANDER FLEMING agt. RICHARD KING is dismist, the Plt. not prosecuting

- The action brought by RICHARD KING against ALEXANDER FLEMING is dismist, the Plt. not prosecuting
- The action brought by ANNE WALKER against GARRARD LYNCH is dismist, the Plt. not prosecuting
- The action brought by JANE PAICE against ANDREW SAULSBERRY is dismist, the Plt. not prosecuting
- The action brought by THOMAS THORNE against JOHN CHAPROONE is dismist, the Plt. not prosecuting
- Nonsuite is granted to JAMES BOURNE against EDWARD BARROW, the Plt. not fileing his Declaration, wch: is ordered to be paid wth: costs of suite als exo

p.   Richmond County Court 4th of October 1705
78   - The action brought by JEREMIAH HOOK agaisnt GEORGE FORELAND is dismist, the Plt. not prosecuting
- Judgment being this day past against the Sherriff for <u>six hundred</u> and sixty foure pounds of tobbo unto PETER EVANS for the non appeareance of EDWARD BARROW att the suite of the said PETER, the said Defendt. being called and faileing to appeare and there being no security returned, Judgment is therefore granted to the Plt. against the Sherriff for the summe aforesaid unless the Defendt. appeare att the next Court and answer the said action
- Judgment being this day past against the Sherriff to PETER EVANS for the non appeareance of EDWARD BARROW att the suite of the said PETER for <u>four hundred</u> and sixty foure pounds of tobbo., upon the motion of the Sherriff, an Attachment is therefore granted him agt. the Estate of the said EDWD. BARROW for the summe aforesd. returnable to the next Court for Judgment
- The action brought by JOHN HAYWARD, Assignee of HENRY SALKELD, against JAMES STORY is dismist, the Plt. not prosecuting
- The action brought by GEORGE RADFORD against JOHN WILSON is dismist, the Plt. not prosecuting
- The action brought by THOMAS WYNN agt. HENRY ASTINE is dismist, the Plt. not prosecuting
- The action brought by WILLIAM SIMMS against JOHN DAVIS is dismist, th Plt. not prosecuting
- The action brought by WILLIAM YATES agt. ROBERT BENT is dismist, the Plt. not prosecuting
- In an action of Debt betweene WILLIAM THORNTON, Plt. and JAMES PHILLIPS, Defendt., for thirteene hundred and fifty two pounds of tobbo. due by Bill, the Defendt. being called and not appeareing nor any security returned, Judgment is therefore granted to the Plt. for the summe aforesaid agt. the Sherriff unless the said Defendt. appeare att the next Court & answer the said action
- Judgment being this day past against the Sherriff for eight hundred and eighty two pounds of tobbo. unto ALEXANDER DONIPHAN for the non appeareance of LAWRENCE YOUNG, upon the motion of the Sherriff an Attachmt. is granted him agt. the Estate of the sd. LAWRENCE YOUNG for the summe aforesd. returnable to the next Court for Judgmt.
- In an action of Debt between ALEXANDER DONIPHAN, Plt. and LAWRENCE YOUNG, Defendt. for eight hundred and eighty two pounds of tobbo. the Defendt. being called and not appeareing nor any security returned, Judgment is

therefore granted to the Plt. for the said summe agt. the Sherriff unless the sd. Defendt. appeare att the next Court & answer the action

p.   Richmond County Court 4th of October 1705
79   - Judgment being this day past against the Sherriff for thirteene hundred and
          fifty pounds of tobbo. unto WILLIAM THORNTON for the non appeareance of
JAMES PHILLIPS att the suite of the said WILLIAM. Upon the motion of the Sherriff, an Attachment is therefore granted unto him for the aforesd. summe of tobbo. against the Estate of the said JAMES PHILLIPS, returnable to the next Court for Judgment
          - The action brought by MARGARETT CAREY, Admrx. of the goods and chattles of RICHARD CAREY, deced., against JAMES RICHISON is dismist, the Plt. not prosecuting
          - The action brought by MARK RYMER against JNO: WISE for fifteene hundred and foure pounds of tobbo. due by Accot., the said Defendt. being called and not appeareing nor any security returned, Judgment is therefore granted to the Plt. against the said Defednt for the summe aforesd. unless the Defendt. appeare att the next Court & answer the said action
          - Judgmt. being this day past against the Sherriff for fifteene hundred and foure pounds of tobbo. unto MARK RYMER for the non appeareance of JOHN WISE att the suite of the said MARK, upon the motion of the Sherriff, an Attachmt. is therefore granted unto him agt. the Estate of the sd. JNO. WISE for the summe aforesaid returnable to the next Court for Judgmt.
          - Judgment is granted to MARK RYMER against EDWARD ROCH for nine hundred and seventy pounds of tobbo. due by Accot., wch: is ordered to be paid with costs of suit als exo
          - Refference is granted in the suite betweene JOHN LOMAX, Plt. and JERE-MIAH STROTHER, Defendt., till next Court
          - Ordered that DAVID BERRICK, JOHN POUND, STANLEY GOWER & GEORGE HALE or any three of them do meet att the House of RICHARD GREENE deced., sometime betweene this and the next Court and do then and there inventory and appraise all and singular the Estate of the said deced., as the same shall be presented to them and make report of theire proceedings therein to the said next Court under theire hands in writeing. Capt. THOMAS BEALE is requested to meet att the time and place aforesaid to administer an Oath to the Appraisers for theire true appraisment of the said deced.'s Estate as also to the Admrx. for the true delivery thereof
          - The action brought by NICHOLAS SMITH agt. JAMES KITCHEN is dismist, the Plt. not prosecuting
          - The action brought by DANLL. HORNEBY agt. EDWARD JEFFEREY in Farnham is dismist, the Plt. being dead
          - The action brought by JOSHUA DAVIS agt. RICHARD TALIAFERRO is dismist, the Plt. not prosecuting
          - Judgmt. is granted to ELIZA: PLEY agt. EDMOND McLYNCHY for twelve hundred pounds of tobbo. wch: is ordered to be paid wth: costs of suite also exo.

p.   Richmond County Court 4th of October 1705
80   - The action brought by ELIZABETH (? KEG) agt. JAMES KITCHEN is

dismist, the Plt. not prosecuting
     - The action brought by DOROTHY STROTHER against HENRY WOOD is dismist, the Plt. not prosecuting
     - In an action of Debt betweene STEVEN SEBASTIN, Plt. and ANTHONY SEALE, Defendt. for thirty good Buck Skins and twelve good Doe Skins due by Bill, the Defendt. being called and not appeareing, Judgmt. is therefore granted to the Plt. against the Sherriff for the number of Skins aforesaid unless he appeare att the next Court & answer the said action
     - Judgment being this day past against the Sherriff for thirty good Buck Skins and twelve good Doe Skins unto STEVEN SEBASTIN for the non appeareance of ANTHONY SEALE att the suite of the said STEVEN, upon the motion of the Sherriff an Attachment is therefore granted unto him against the Estate of ANTHONY SEALE for the number of Skinns aforesd. returnable to the next Court for Judgment
     - In an action of Debt betweene STEPHEN SEBASTIN, Plt. and ANTHO: SEALE, Defendt., for thirty good Buck Skins and ten good Doe Skins and Ten pounds Sterl. damage, the Defendt. being called and not appeareing, Justment is therefore granted to the Plt. agt. the Sherriff for the number of Skinns and damage aforesd. unless the Defendt. appeare att the next Court & answer the said action
     - Judgment being this day past against the Sherriff for thirty good Buck Skins and ten good Doe Skins and ten pounds Sterl. damage unto STEVEN SEBASTIN for the non appeareance of ANTHONY SEALE att the suite of the said STEVEN, upon the motion of the Sherriff, an Attachment is granted unto him against the Estate of the said ANTHONY SEALE for the number of skinns and damage aforesaid returnable to the next Court for Judgment
     - Nonsuite is granted against EDWARD JEFFEREYS for his non appeareance in the action brought by him agt. ROBERT KING, and it is ordered that he pay the same with costs als exo
     - The action brought by ALEXANDER DONIPHAN agt. JNO: ELKYNS is dismist, the Plt. not prosecuting
     - The action brought by Colo. JNO: BATTAILE agt. ALEXR. SINKLER is dismist, the Plt not prosecuting
     - The action brought by Colo. JNO: BATTAILE agt. WILLIAM SMITH is dismist, the Plt. not prosecuting

p.   Richmond County Court 4th of October 1705
81   - Nonsuite is granted to PETER EVANS for the non appeareance of JOHN
       JEWELL wch: is ordered to be paid wth: costs of suit als exo
     - The action brought by JOHN WALKER against JOSEPH BELFIELD is dismist, the Plt. not prosecuting
     - The action brought by THOMAS PANNELL agt. JOHN GREENE is dismist the Plt. not prosecuting
     - The action brought by WILLIAM WILLIS agt. WM. COOMES is dismist, the Plt. not prosecuting
     - The action brought by NICHOLAS SMITH agt. JEREMIAH HOOKE is dismist, the Plt. not prosecuting
     - The action brought by KATHERINE GWYN, Exrx. of the Last Will and Testament of Majr. DAVID GWYN, agt. CORNELIUS COMISKEY is dismist, ye Plt.

not prosecuting

    - The action brought by PATIENCE NAYLER, Exrx. of the Last Will and Testament of AVERY NAYLER, agt. WM. SMITH, Shoemaker, is dismist, the Plt. not prosecuting

    - The action of Case betweene PATIENCE NAYLER, Exrx. of the Last Will and Testament of AVERY NAYLER, deced., Plt. and JOSEPH BELFIELD, Defendt. for two thousand three hundred and ninety three pounds of tobbo. and caske due by Bill, the Defendt. being called and not appeareing nor any security returned, Judgment is therefore granted to the Plt. against the Sherriff for the sd. summe unless the Defendt. appeare att the next Court and answer the said action

    - Judgmt. being this day past against the Sherriff for two thousand three hundred and ninety three pounds of tobbo. unto PATIENCE NAYLER, Exrx. of the Last Will and Testament of AVERY NAYLER, for the non appeareance of JOSEPH BELFIELD at the suite of the said PATIENCE, upon the motion of the Sherriff, Attachment is therefore granted unto him agt. the Estate of JOSEPH BELFIELD for ye summe aforesd. returnable to the next Court for Judgment

    - The action brought by SISLEY JORDAN agt. JNO: IKEY is dismist, the Plt. not prosecuting

    - Nonsuite is granted to PETER EVANS for the non appeareance of THO. MADDISTONE wch: is ordered to be paid with costs als exo

    - The action brought by CHARLES BARBER, High Sherriff of Richmond County against JNO: STEELE, Mercht., is dismist, the Plt. not prosecuting

    - Ordered that the Jury be paid theire charges in the suite betweene HENRY ASTINE, Plt. and GEO: RADFORD, Defendt.

    - JOHN POUND being subpaencd as an Evidence for HENRY ASTINE in the suite betweene him and GEORGE RADFORD & having therein attended seven dayes hath order granted against the sd. HENRY ASTINE for allowance for the same according to Law als exo

p.   <u>Richmond County Court 4th of October 1705</u>

82   - JOHN WILSON being subpaened as an Evidence for HENRY ASTINE in a suite betweene him and GEORGE RADFORD and therein having attended seven days, hath order granted against HENRY ASTINE for allowance for the same according to Law als exo

    - The Probate of the Last Will and Testament of JAMES SAMFORD continued

    - The action brought by Majr. WILLIAM ROBINSON against NEHEMIAH JONES is continued till next Court by consent

    - The Attachment granted to THOMAS WHITE agt. the Estate of THOMAS DEACUS is continued till next Court

    - The Attachment granted to THOMAS WHITE agt. the Estate of ROBERT PAYNE is continued till next Court

    - In an action of Case between JOSEPH TAYLOE, Plt. and CHARLES DODSON, JUNR., Defendt., for three thousand two hundred pounds of tobbo. damage, the Defendt. being called and not appeareing nor any security returned, Judgmt. is therefore granted to the Plt. against the Sherriff for the said summe unless the Defendt. appeare att the next Court and answer the said action

    - Judgment being this day past against the Sherriff for three thousand two hundred pounds of tobbo. damage unto JOSEPH TAYLOE for the non appeareance of CHARLES DODSON, JUNR. att the suite of the said JOSEPH, upon the motion of the Sherriff an Attachment is granted him against the Estate of CHARLES DODSON for the sume aforesd. returnable to the next Court for Judgmt.

- In an action of Debt betweene ELIZABETH WOODWARD, Admrx. of all & singular the goods and chattles of WILLIAM WOODWARD, late of LANCASTER County, deced., Plt. and CORMACK McKENNY, Defendt., for seven hundred pounds of tobbo. and caske, the Defendt. being called and not appeareing, Judgment is therefore granted to the Plt. agt. the Sherriff for the said summe unless the Defendt. appeare att the next Court & answer the said action

- Judgment being this day past against the Sherriff for seven hundred pounds of tobbo. unto ELIZA: WOODWARD, Admrx. of all and singular the goods and chattles of WILLIAM WOODWARD, late of LANCASTER County, deced., for the non appeareance of CORMACK McKENNY att the suite of the said ELIZABETH, upon the motion of the Sherriff an Attachment is therefore granted unto him agt. the Estate of said CORMACK McKENNY for the summe aforesd. returnable to the next Court for Judgmt.

p.   Richmond County Court 4th of October 1705
83   - In an action of Trespass betweene WILLIAM BARBER and JOYCE his Wife, Plts. and SAMLL. SAMFORD, Planter, of the Parish of Farnham and County of Richmond, Defendt., for one hundred pounds Sterl. damage, the Defendt. being called and not appeareing, Judgment is therefore granted to the Plts. agt. the Sherriff for the summe aforesaid unless the Defendt. appeare att the next Court and answer the said action

- Judgment being this day past against the Sherriff for one hundred pounds Sterl. damage unto WILLIAM BARBER and JOYCE his Wife for the non appeare-ance of SAMLL. SAMFORD, Planter of the Parish of Northfarnham and County of Richmond, upon the motion of the Sherriff, an Attachment is therefore granted unto him against the Estate of SAMLL. SAMFORD for the sume aforesd. returnable to the next Court for Judgment

- Nonsuite is granted to JOHN DALTON and MARY his Wife, Admrx. of WILLIAM BROCKENBROUGH, deced., for the non appeareance of JOSHUA YOUNG wch: is ordered to be paid with costs of suite als exo

- Order against the Sherriff is granted to THOMAS MACKEY for the non appeareance of JAMES PHILLIPS according to Declaration

- Attachment is thereupon granted to the Sherriff returnable, &c.

- The action brought by JOB HAMMOND agt. FRANCIS LYNCH is dismist, the Plt. not prosecuting

- The action brought by BENJAMIN DEVERELL agt. THOMAS HARPER is dismist, the Plt. not prosecuting

- The action brought by WILLIAM LAMBERT agt. CHARLES DODSON is dismist, the Plt. not prosecuting

- The action brought by JOHN WHITE agt. WILLIAM SMITH, Shoemaker, is dismsit, the Plt. not prosecuting

- The action of Case brought by JNO: WHITE agt. WM. SMITH, Shoemaker, is dismist, the Plt. not prosecuting

- The action brought by SAMLL. GODWIN agt. JNO. WORDEN is dismist,

the Plt. not prosecuting
    - The action brought by CATHERINE GWYN, Exrx. of the goods & chattles of
Majr. DAVID GWYN, deced., against JOSEPH RUSSELL is continued till next Court
    - In an action of Debt betweene EDWARD JEFFEREYS, Plt. and THOMAS
FINWICK, Defendt., for nine hundred and seventy six pounds of tobbo., the Defendt.
being called and not appeareing, Judgmt. is therefore granted to the Plt. against the

p.   Richmond County Court 4th of October 1705
84   Sherriff for the summe aforesd. unless the Defendt. appeare att the next
        Court and answer the sd. action
    - Judgment being this day past against the Sherriff unto EDWARD JEF-
FEREYS for the non appeareance of THOMAS FINWICK att the suite of said
EDWARD for nine hundred and seventy six pounds of tobbo., upon the motion of the
Sherriff, an Attachment is therefore granted unto him agt. the Estate of the sd.
THOMAS for the said summe returnable to the next Court for Judgment
    - In an action of Case between ANDREW SAULSBERRY, Plt. and PETER
EVANS, Defendt., for five hundred and eighty five pounds of tobbo due by Accot., the
Defendt. being called and not appeareing, Judgmt. is therefore granted to the Plt.
against the Sherriff for the summe aforesd. unless the Defendt. appeare att the next
Court and answer the said action
    - Judgment being this day past against the Sherriff for five hundred eighty five
pounds of tobbo. unto ANDREW SAULSBERRY for the non appeareance of PETER
EVANS att the suite of the said ANDREW, upon the motion of the Sherriff an
Attachment is granted him agt. the Estate of PETER EVANS for the summe aforesaid returnable to the next Court for Judgment
    - In an action of Debt betweene ANDREW SAULSBERRY, Plt. and PETER
EVANS, Defendt., for two hundred pounds of tobbo. due by Bill, the Defendt. being
called and not appeareing, Judgment is therefore granted to the Plt. agt. the Sherriff
for the sume aforesd. unless the Defendt. appeare att the next Court and answer the
said action
    - Judgment being this day past against the Sherrif unto ANDREW SAULS-
BERRY for the non appeareance of PETER EVANS att the suite of sd. ANDREW for
two hundred pounds of tobbo, upon the motion of the Sherriff, an Attachment is
therefore granted him agt the Estate of PETER EVANS for the said summe returnable to the next Court for Judgment
    - The action brought by the Queene and JOHN BATTAILE agt. THOMAS
DEACUS is dismist, the Plts. not prosecuting
    - The action brought by DANLL. HORNBY agt. EDWARD JEFFEREYS is
dismist, the Plt. not prosecuting
    - The action brought by JOSHUA LAWSON, Admr. of THOMAS PARKER,
agt. JNO. SUGGITT and ELIZA. SUGGITT, Exrs. of the Last Will and Testa-ment of
JOHN SUGGITT, deced., is dismist, the Plt. not prosecuting
    - The action brought by MATHEW BURROWS agt. JOSEPH BELFIELD is
dismist, the Plt. not prosecuting

p.   Richmond County Court 4th of October 1705
85   - In an action of Debt betweene EDWARD NEWTON, Plt. and DANLL.

McGWYRE, Defendt. for foure hundred and fifty pounds of tobbo. and three barrells of Indian Corne, the Defendt. being called and not appeareing, Judgmt. is therefore granted to the Plt. agt. JOSEPH BELFIELD, Security returned for his appeareance, for the summe aforesaid unless the Defendt. appeare att the next Court and answer the said action

    - The action brought by NICHOLAS CHRISTOPHER against JOHN RICHESON, is dismist the Plt. not prosecuting

    - The action brought by WILLIAM PANNELL agt. GARRARD LYNCH is dismist, the Plt. not prosecuting

    - The action brought by JOSHUA DAVIS against EDWARD TAYLER is dismist, the Plt. not prosecuting

    - The action brought by WILLIAM DICKENSON agt. LEWIS GRIFFIS is dismist, the Plt. not prosecuting

    - The action brought by LEWIS GRIFFIS against WILLIAM DICKENSON is dismist, the Plt. not prosecuting

    - Nonsuite is granted to THOMAS GRIMSLEY for the non appeareance of JUSTIN STEELE wch. is ordered to be paid wth: costs of suit als exo

    - In an action of Debt betweene ROBERT PAYNE, Plt. and DANIELL MERRITT, Defendt., for one thousand four hundred sixty eight pounds of tobbo. due by Bill, and the Defendt. being returned by the Sherriff a copy left and not appeareing, Attachment is therefore granted to the Plt. agt. the Estate of the Defendt. for the afaoresd. summe returnable to the next Court for Judgmt.

    - In an action of Debt betweene ROBERT PAYNE, Plt. and ABRAHAM HANNESON, Defendt. for two thousand pounds of tobbo. damage, the Defendt. being called and not appeareing, Judgmt. is therefore granted to the Plt. against THOMAS PANNELL, security returned for the said summe unless the Defendt appeare att the next Court and answer the said action

    - In an action of Case betweene ROBERT PAYNE, Plt. and ABRAHAM HANNESON, Defendt. for foure hundred pounds of tobbo. due by Bill, the Defendt. being called and not appeareing, Judgmt. is therefore granted to the Plt. for the summe aforesaid against THOMAS PANNELL, security returned for his appeareance, unless ye sd. Defendt. appeare att the next Court and answer the said action

    - Refference is granted in the suite betweene SYMON PASCOE, Plt. and THOMAS HARPER, Defendt. till next Court

    - The suite if Chancery commenced by AVERY DYE by his nearest Friend & Father, ARTHUR DYE, against PATIENCE NAYLOR, Exrx. of the Last Will and Testament of AVERY NAYLER, deced., is dismist, the Plt. not prosecuting

    - The action brought by JAMES STROTHER agt. JOHN (? CLEA) is dismist, the Plt. not prosecuting

p.   Richmond County Court 4th of October 1705
86   - The action brought by WILLIAM SMITH, Tanner, agt. WILLIAM YATES is dismist, the Plt. not prosecuting

    - The action brought by WILLIAM DACRE against JOHN WHITE is dismist, the Plt. not prosecuting

    - WILLIAM DACRE brought his action in this Court against THOMAS SCURLOCK for twenty pounds Sterl. damage by meanes of his, the sd. Defendt., takeing, rideing away and unlawfully useing and labouring one flea bitten gelding of the value of ten pounds Sterl., being the proper goods and chattles of him the sd. Plt., to which the Defendt. in his proper person comes into Court and pleads Not Guilty. Whereupon a Jury was impannelled and sworne to trye the matter in issue by name

ROBERT PAYNE	JNO. SETTLE	JAMES TRENT
JOHN BOWEN	JNO. GRIMSLEY	JOB HAMMOND, JUNR.
ALEXR. FLEMING	WM. YATES	PETER EVANS
JNO: KELLY	JAMES SUGGITT	JNO. WILLIS, JUNR.

who being returned brought in for Verdict; We of the Jury do find for the Plt. twenty shillings damage, wch: Verdict upon the motion of the Plt. is ordered to be recorded and that the Defendt. do pay the same wth: costs als exo

- This day JAMES COWARD confest Judgment to THOMAS REEVE for two hundred pounds of tobbo. wch: is ordered to be paid wth: costs of suite als exo

- In an action of Debt betweene JAMES COWARD, Plt. and GEORGE BLEWFORD, Defendt. for seven hundred & fourty pounds of tobbo. due by Bill, the Defendt. being called and not appeareing, Judgment is therefore granted to the Plt. agt. ALEXANDER FLEMING, security returned for his appeareance, for the said summe unless the Defendt. appeare att the next Court & answer the said action

- In an action of Case betweene EDWARD JONES, Plt. and JOHN BROWNE, Defendt., for one thousand pounds of tobbo. damage, the Defendt. being called and not appeareing, Judgment is therefore gratned to the Plt. against MARTIN SHERMAN, security returned for his appeareance for the said summe unless the Defendt. appeare att the next Court and answer the said action

- In an action of Debt betweene Doctor ROBERT CLARKE, Assignee of JOHN LYNDSEY, Plt. and JOHN DALTON and MARY his Wife, Defendts., for five hundred and twenty foure pounds of tobbo. and three thillings in money due by Bill, the Defendts. being called and not appeareing, nor any security returned, Judgment is therefore granted to the Plt. agt. the Sherriff for the sume aforesaid unless the Defendts. appeare att the next Court and answer the said action

p. Richmond County Court 4th of October 1705
87   - Judgment being this day past against the Sherriff for five hundred and
       twenty foure pounds of tobbo.unto ROBERT CLARKE, Assignee of JOHN
LYNSEY for the non appeareance of JOHN DALTON and MARY his Wife att the suite of the said ROBERT, upon the motion of the Sherriff an Attachment is granted him agt. the Estate of the sd. JOHN & MARY returnable to the next Court for Judgment

- The action of Debt between WILLIAM HANKS, Admr. of WM. HANKS, deced., Plt. and HENRY JENNINGS, Defendt. for eight hundred and twenty five pounds of tobbo. the Defendt. being called and not appeareing nor any security being returned, Judgmt. is therefore granted to the Plt. agt. the Sherriff for the summe aforesaid unless the Defendt. appeare att next Court and answer the said action

- Judgment being this day past against the Sherriff unto WM. HANKS, Admr. of WM. HANKS, deced., for the non appeareance of HENRY JENNINGS att the suite of said WILLIAM for eight hundred and twenty five pounds of tobbo, upon the motion of the Sherriff an Attachment is granted him agt. the Estate of HENRY JENNINGS returnable to the next Court for Judgment

- In an action of Debt betweene WILLIAM HANKS, Admr. of WM. HANKS, deced., Plt. against JAMES PEARSON, Defendt. for two hundred thirty five pounds of tobbo. due by Bill, the Defendt. being called and not appeareing, nor any security returned, Judgment is therefore granted to the Plt. agt. the Sherriff for the said summe unless the Defendt. appeare att the next Court and answer the said action

- Judgment being this day past against the Sherriff for two hundred & thirty five pounds of tobb. unto WILLIAM HANKS, Admr. of WM. HANKS, deced., for the non appeareance of JAMES PEARSON att the suite of the sd. WM., upon the motion of the Sherriff an Attachment is granted him against the Estate of JAMES PEARSON for the said summe returnable to the next Court for Judgment

- In an action of Case between ALEXANDER CAMBELL, Plt. and HENRY JENNINGS, Defendt. for foure hundred and fifty pounds of tobbo. due by Accot., the Defendt. being called and not appeareing nor any security returned, Judgment is therefore granted to the Plt. against the Sherriff for the summe aforesaid unless the Defendt. appeare att the next Court and answer the said action

- Judgment being this day past against the Sherriff unto ALEXANDER CAMBELL for the non appeareance of HENRY JENNINGS att the suite of said ALEXR., for foure hundred and fifty pounds of tobbo, upon the motion of the Sherriff an Attachment is therefore granted him agt. the Estate of HENRY JENNINGS for ye said summe, returnable to the next Court for Judgment

- The action brought by HENRY JENNINGS agt. ALEXANDER CAMBELL is dismist, the Plt. not prosecuting

- The action brought by DAVID WILLIAMS agt, EDWARD JONES is dismist the Plt. not prosecuting

p.   Richmond County Court 4th of October 1705
88   - The action brought by EDWARD JONES against DAVID WILLIAMS is dismist, the Plt. not prosecuting

- The action brought by EDWARD JONES agt. THOMAS LLOYD, Taylor, is dismist, the Plt. not prosecuting

- In an Ejectione Firma depending in this Court between WILLIAM BARBER, Plt. and THOMAS GLASCOCK, Defendt., for the Defendts. (   ) from one certaine Plantation wth: the appurtenances & two hundred acres of Land sitaute in the Parish of Farnham and County of Richmond wch: JNO: TARPLEY, Gent., did demise to him the sd. WILLIAM BARBER, for a terme of yeares not yett expired and now or late in the possession of WILLIAM AKERS, MANUS MACKLACKLIN having made Oath that ht served WM. AKERS, the tenant in possession of the land and premises afore-sd. wth: a copy of the Plt.'s Declaration in this behalfe and the notice thereon endorsed Ordered that unless WM. AKERS, tenant in possession or those under whome he claymes having due notice of this Order by the Sherriff of this County do appeare att the next Court held for this County, confess lease entry and ouster, and enter him-selfe Defendt. in the roome and stead of THOMAS GLASCOCK and insist only upon the Tryall of the title, Judgment do pass against him by default

- In an action of Case betweene Doctor ROBERT CLARKE, Plt. and SAMLL. SAMFORD, Executr. of JAMES SAMFORD, Defendt., for sixteene hundred & fifty pounds of tobbo. due by Accot. the Defendt. being called and not appeareing, Judgment is therefore granted to the Plt. agt. GYLES WEBB, security returned for his appeareance, unless the Defendt. appeare att the next Court and answer the said action

    - The action brought by WILLIAM LAMBERT agt. WALTER WRIGHT is dismist, the Plt. not prosecuting

    - The action brought by RICHARD DODSON agt. ABRAHAM DALE is dismist, the Plt. not prosecuting

    - In an action of Case betweene JAMES COWARD, Plt. and RICHARD KING Defendt., for two and twenty hundred & fifty pounds of tobbo. due by Accot., the Defendt. being called and not appeareing nor any security returned, Judgmt. is therefore ganted to the Plt. agt. the Sherriff for the said summe unless the Defendt. appeare att the next Court and answer the said action

    - Judgment being this day past against the Sherriff for two and twenty hundred and fifty pounds of tobbo. unto JAMES CAWARD, for the non appeareance of RICHARD KING at the suite of the said JAMES, upon the motion of the Sherriff an Attachment is granted him agt. the Estate of the Defendt. for the summe aforesaid returnable to the next Court for Judgmt.

p.   <u>Richmond County Court 4th of October 1705</u>

89   - The action brought by GEORGE PHLLLIPS against ROBERT LEGG is dismist, the Plt. not prosecuting

    - The action brought by DANLL. MERRITT agt. PHILLIP BROWNE is dismist, the Plt. not prosecuting

    - The action of Case brought by DANLL. MERRITT agt. PHILLIP BROWNE is dismist, the Plt. not prosecuting

    - Nonsuite is granted to WILLIAM SMITH, Tanner, agt. ALEXANDER SINKLER, the said ALEXR. not fileing his Declaration in time, and it is ordered that he pay the same wth: costs of suite als exo

    - The action brought by GEORGE RADFORD against JAMES NELSON is dismist, the Plt. not prosecuting

    - The action bought by KATHERINE GWYN, Exrx. of the Last Will and Testament of Majr. DAVID GWYN, agt. JAMES LYNDSEY is dismist, the Plt. not prosecuting

    - In an action of Detinue betweene JOHN KELLEY, Plt. and JAMES TRENT, Defendt. for three thousand pounds of tobbo. damage and one bay stone Horse branded with floure de luce, the Defendt. being called and not appeareing nor any security returned, Judgmt. is therefore granted agt. the Sherriff for the Horse and damage aforesd. unless the Defendt. appeare att the next Court and answer the said action

    - Judgment being this day past against the Sherriff for three thousand pounds of tobbo. damage and one ay stone Horse branded with floure de luce unto JOHN KELLY for the non appeareance of JAMES TRENT att the suite of JOHN KELLY, upon the motion of the Sherriff an Attachment is granted him agt. the Estate of JAMES TRENT for the Horse and damage aforesd. returnable to the next Court for Judgmt.

    - The action brought by JAMES NELSON agt. ARTHUR DYE, Defendt. is dismist, the Plt. not prosecuting

    - Refference granted in the suite betweene MARY BURK, Plt. and ROBERT KING, Defendt. till next Court

    - In an action of Case betweene JOSHUA DAVIS, Plt. and RICHARD TALIA-FERRO, Defendt., for fifty pounds Sterl. damage and the produce of one Still and

Worme containeing eighty odd gallons & of the value of twenty foure pounds Sterl., prime cost sold by the Defendt in BARBADOES and to be returned in good Rumm & Suggar att the price there current, and the Defendt. being called and not appeareing, Judgment is therefore granted to the Plt. against the Sherriff for the produce of the Still and damage aforesaid unless the Defendt. appeare att the next Court and answer the said action

- Judgment being this day past agt. the Sherriff unto JOSHUA DAVIS for the non appeareance of RICHARD TALIAFERRO att the suite of the said JOSHUA, for fifty pounds Sterling damage and the produce of one Still and Worme containeing eighty odd gallons & of the value of twenty foure pounds Sterl. prime costs sold by RICHARD TALIAFERRO in BARBADOES and to be returned in good Rumm and Suggar att the price current there, upon the motion of the Sherriff, an Attachmt. is granted him agt. the Estate of RICHARD TALIAFERRO for the produce of the Still & damage aforesd. returnable to the next Court for Judgmt.

p.   Richmond County Court 4th of October 1705
90   - In an action of Case betweene the Church Wardens of St. Mary's Parish, Plts. and WILLIAM WILLIS, Defendt., for what charges the said Parish hath been att in the keeping of KATHERINE HENDERKIN, the Defendt. being called and not appeareing, Judgmt. is therefore granted to the Plts. against JNO: WILLIS, security returned for his appeareance, for the charges aforesaid unless the Defendt. appeare att the next Court and answer the said action

- This day JAMES PHILLIPS acknowledged a Deed of Land to THOMAS PANNELL wch: is ordered to be recorded

- This day JAMES PHILLIPS confest Judgment to THOMAS MACKEY for five hundred pounds of tobbo., wch: is ordered to be paid wth: costs of suite als exo

- The Ejectione Firma brought by DOMINICK BENNEHAN agt. ROWLAND LAWSON is continued till next Court

- The action brought by JOHN HARPER agt. THOMAS HUGHES is dismist, the Plt. not prosecuting

- The action of Case brought by JOHN HARPER agt. THOMAS HUGHES is dismist, the Plt. not prosecuting

- The action of Trespass brought by LAWRENCE PRESCOTT agt. JUDITH FOX is dismist, the Plt. not prosecuting

- The action of Trespass brought by LAWRENCE FOX against RICHARD DOWDALL is dismist, the Plt. not prosecuting

- The action of Theft brought by JUDITH FOX agt. JANE PRESCOTT is dismist, the Plt. not prosecuting

- The action of Slander brought by JUDITH FOX agt. JANE PRESCOTT is dismist, the Plt. not prosecuting

- The action brought by SARAH TILLERY agt. JNO. (SELL-------) is dismist, the Plt. not prosecuting

- In an action of Debt betweene ROBERT GIBSON and RUTH his Wife, JOSEPH BELFIELD and FRANCES his Wife, Admrx. of the goods and chattles of MOTRON WRIGHT, deced., Plts. against CHARLES DODSON, JUNR., Defendt., for foure hundred and fifteene pounds of tobbo. the Defendt. being called and not appeareing, Judgment is therefore granted to the Plts. for the summe aforesd. agt. JOSHUA STONE security returned for his appearance, unless the Defendt. appeare att the next Court and answer the said action

    - The action brought by JNO: MILLS agt. ROBERT BARLOW is dismist, the Plt. not prosecuting

    - The action brought by JOHN BOWEN agt. JAMES LYNDSEY is dismist, the Plt. not prosecuting

    - In an action of Debt betweene THOMAS GRIFFIN, Plt. and JOHN BROWN

p.   <u>Richmond County Court 4th of October 1705</u>

91   Defendt., for six hundred and forty five pounds of tobbo. due by Bill, the Defendt. being called and not appeareing nor any security returned, Judgment is therefore granted to the Plt. agt. the Sherriff for the said summe unless the Defendt. appeare att the next Court and answer the said action

    - Judgment being this day past against the Sherriff for six hundred and forty five pounds of tobbo. unto THOMAS GRIFFIN for the non appeareance of JOHN BROWN att the suite of said THOMAS, upon the motion of the Sherriff, an Attachment is granted him agt, the Estate of JOHN BROWNE for the summe aforesaid returnable to the next Court for Judgment

    - In an action of Debt betweene THOMAS GRIFFIN and WILLIAM MARSHALL, Defendt., for foure hundred and ninety pounds of tobbo. due by Bill, the Defendt. being returned by the Sherriff a Coppy left and not appeareing, an Attachment is granted the Plt. against the Estate of the Defendt. for the summe aforesaid returnable to the next Court for Judgmt.

    - In an action of Debt betweene THOMAS GRIFFIN and JOHN SETTLE, for five hundred and thirty pounds of tobbo., the Defendt. being called and not appeareing nor any security returned, Judgmt. is therefore granted to the Plt. against the Sherriff for the said summe unless the Defendt. appeare att the next Court and answer the said action

    - Judgment being this day past agt. the Sherriff for five hundred and thirty pounds of tobbo. unto THOMAS GRIFFIN for the non appearance of JOHN SETTLE att the suite of said THOMAS, upon the motion of the Sherriff an Attachment is granted him agt. the Estate of JOHN SETTLE for the summe aforesaid returnable to the next Court for Judgment

    - In an action of Debt betweene GOWEN CORBIN, Plt and JOSEPH LEWRIGHT, Defendt. for seven hundred pounds of tobbo. & caske due by Bill, the Defendt. being returned by the Sherriff by Coppy left, and not appeareing, Attachment is granted to the Plt. agt. the Estate of the Defendt. for the said summe returnable to the next Court for Judgment

    - Nonsuite is granted WILLIAM SMITH, Tanner, for the non appeareance of WILLIAM YATES, wch: is ordered to be paid wth: costs of suite als exo

    - The action brought by EDWARD TURBERVILL against ROBERT KING is dismist, the Plt. not prosecuting

    - The action brought by ABIGAIL TRIPLETT agt. WILLIAM PILKINTON is dismist, the Plt. not prosecuting

    - The action brought by PAUL MICOU agt. JNO. DUCKER is dismist, the Plt. not prosecuting

    - The action brought by PAUL MICOU agt. JAMES STORY is dismist, the Plt. not prosecuting

- The action brought by JOSEPH BELFIELD agt. PATRICK TIFFY is continued till next Court

p.   Richmond County Court 4th of October 1705
92   - The action brought by THOMAS DICKENSON agt. PETER BENNETT is dismist, the Plt. not prosecuting
- The action brought by THOMAS DICKENSON agt. JOHN BURGER is dismist, the Plt. not prosecuting
- The action brought by ABIGAIL TRIPLETT agt. WILLIAM PILKINTON is dismist, the Plt. not prosecuting
- Judgment renewed by Scire Facias to JOHN SETTLE against ROBERT TAYLER for twenty shillings Sterl. due upon a Judgment of this Court dated Febry. the third 1703, wch. is ordered to be paid wth: former & present costs als exo
- Upon the Petition of HUGH FRENCH, one of the Sons of HUGH FRENCH, late of this County, deced., by WILLIAM TRIPLETT his prochein amy agt. JOHN SOMERVELL and MARGT. his Wife, Exrx. of the Last Will & Testament of the sd. HUGH FRENCH, deced., setting forth that the said HUGH FRENCH did by his Last Will and Testament give and devise to each of his Sons a feather bed & furniture, sheets, a horse & five thousand pounds of tobbo.& a pott & a frying pann. The Defendts. being summoned to shew cause if any they could why they rendered not unto him, the Plt., his Legacy aforesd., and faileing to appeare, Judgment is therefore granted unto him agt. the sd. JNO: & MARGT., Exrx. as aforesaid, for the aforesaid Legacy so given unto him by the Will of his Father, deced., unless they appeare att the next Court and shew cause to the contrary
- Ordered that JOHN GRIMSLEY be paid by THOMAS GRIMSLEY for three days attendances according to Act being by him subpaened as an evidence in the suite betweene JUSTIN STEELE, Plt. and the sd. THOMAS GRIMSLEY, Defendt., als exo
- JOHN MINIFY hath Order granted for two days attendance according to Law agt. WILLIAM YATES as an evidence in the suite betweene him and WILLIAM SMITH, Tanner, als exo
- JOHN PALMER hath Order granted for two days attendance according to Law agt. WILLIAM YATES as an evidence in the suite betweene WILLIAM YATES, Plt., and WILLIAM SMITH, Tanner, Defendt., als exo.
- MARGERY PALMER hath Order granted for two days attendance according to Law agt. WILLIAM YATES as an evidence in the suite betweene him and WILLIAM SMITH, Tanner, als exo
- WILLIAM MARSHALL having attended two days to prove the Will of CHARLES TEBO hath Order granted for allowance for the same agt. FRANCES TEBO according to Law als exo
- RICHARD TANKERSLEY having attended two days to prove the Will of

p.   Richmond County Court 4th of October 1705
93   CHARLES TEBO, deced., hath Order granted for allowance for the same against FRANCES TEBO als exo
- The Order to summon JAMES BIDDLECOMB upon presentment of the Grand Jury against him for entertaineing ZACHARIAH NICHOLLS and the woman

commonly called MARY MALADY continued till next Court

    - The Order to summon ZACHARIAH NICHOLLS and MARY MALADY upon suspition of theire living in adultery together is continued till the next Court

    The Order to summon EDWARD BARROW upon the presentment of the Grand Jury against him for suffereing unlawfull toll to be taken at his Mill and not having measures and toll dishes according to Law, continued till next Court

    - Order to summon MARGARETT, late Servant to JOSEPH BELFIELD, now living at JOHN FENNER's upon presentment of the Grand Jury agt. her for beareing a Molatto bastard continued till next Court

    - Order to summon JAMES LYNDSEY of Sittenburne Parish upon presentment of the Grand Jury agt. him for not goeing to Church for two moneths together, continued till next Court

    - The Order to summon JAMES WILSON of Farnham Parish upon presentment of the Grand Jury agt. him for concealeing a Tythable continued till next Court

    - The Order to summon EDWARD JEFFEREYS, Ordinary Keeper, upon presentment of the Grand Jury against him sweareing three Oaths continued till next Court

    - The Order to summon EDWARD JEFFEREYS, Ordinary Keeper, upon presentment by the Grand Jury agt. him for not selling Drink in lawfull measures is continued till next Court

    - The Order to summon JAMES STEPHENSON of Farnham Parish upon presentment of the Grand Jury agt. him for not goeing to Church for halfe a yeare together continued till next Court

    - The Order to summon CHRISTOPHER JONES of Sittenburne Parish upon presentment by the Grand Jury against him for carrying a nett on the Sabbath Day is continued till next Court

    - The Court is adjourned till the first Wednesday in December next

p. 94   - Att a Court held for Richmond County the 5th day of December 1705

Present

Lieut. Colo. SAMLL. PEACHEY	Capt. THOMAS BEALE
Majr. WM. ROBINSON	Capt. CHARLES BARBER
Capt. ALEXR. DONIPHAN	Mr. JOSHUA DAVIS Justices

    - A new Commission of the Peace being this day opened and publickly read and Dedimus Potestatem for administering the Oathes, &c., to the Gentlemen therein named Justices of the Peace for this County, in pursuance whereof Capt. CHARLES BARBER and Mr. JOSHUA DAVIS having first administered the Oathes appointed by Act of Parliament instead of the Oathes of Allegiance and Supremacy unto Lieut. Colo. SAMLL. PEACHEY & Capt. ALEXANDER DONIPHAN (who likewise signed the Test) did also administer to them the Oath of a Justice of the Peace, after which they, the said SAMUELL PEACHEY and ALEXANDER DONIPHAN, did administer the Oathes appointed by Act of Parliament instead of the Oathes of Allegiance and Supremacie and the Oath of duely executing the Office of a Justice unto Majr. WM. ROBINSON, Capt. CHARLES BARBER, Mr. JOSHUA DAVIS, Mr. EDWARD BARROW, Mr. NICHOLAS SMITH & Mr. JOSEPH DEEKE, who likewise signed the Test

-----

Att a Court held for Richmond County the 5th day of Xber 1705

Present

Lieut. Colo. SAMLL. PEACHEY	Mr. JOSHUA DAVIS
Majr. WILLIAM ROBINSON	Mr. EDWD. BARROW
Capt. ALEXANDER DONIPHAN	Mr. NICHO: SMITH
Capt. CHARLES BARBER	Mr. JOSEPH DEEKE Justices

- This day the Inventory and Appraisment of the Estate of RICHARD GREENE being presented to this Court by SAMLL. BAYLY, the same is ordered to be recorded

- This day the Inventory and Appraisment of the Estate of DANIELL HORNEBY being presented to this Court by THOMAS SUGGITT is ordered to be recorded

- This day the Inventory and Appraisment of the Estate of WILLIAM HANKS being presented to this Court by WILLIAM HANKS, JUNR., is ordered to be recorded

p.   Richmond County Court 5th of December 1705
95   - It appeareing to this Court that JOHN FAGAN, Servant to JOHN SUG-
GITT, late deceased, had absented himselfe out of his said Masters service the space of eight days and that he had expended the summe of six hundred pounds of tobbo. to procure him againe. Ordered that he serve ELIZABETH SUGGITT, Exrx. of the said deced., his present Mrs., or her assignes the terme of eight moneths after his time by Indenture Custome or otherwise be expired

- Upon the motion of WILLIAM PHILLIPS and BARTHOLOMEW DAWSEY, ordered that Capt. JOHN CRASKE, HENRY BRUCE and JAMES INGO or any two of them, sometime betweene this and the next Court do meet att the Hosue where JAMES SPENDERGRASS, late deced., did live and do then and there inventory and appraise all and singular the Estate of the said JAMES as shall be presented to their view and make report of theire proceedings therein to the next Court under their hands in writing

- Mr. EDWARD BARROW is requested to administer an Oath to the Apprai-sers for theire true appraisment of the said deced.'s Estate as also to WILLIAM PHILLIPS and BARTHOLOMEW DAWSEY for the true delivery thereof

- Ordered that JAMES SPENDERGRASS, Son of JAMES SPENDERGRASS deced., do continue wth: BARTHOLOMEW DAWSEY and that the said BARTHOLO-MEW do take him into his care and tuitiion till he shall be otherwise ordered by the Court

- Ordered that JOHN SPENDERGRASS, Son of JAMES SPENDERGRASS, deced., do continue wth: WILLIAM PHILLIPS and that the said WILLIAM do take him into his care and tuition till it shall be otherwise ordered by this Court

- This day RICHARD BRAMHAM acknowledged a Deed for Land to HENRY WEBSTER which is ordered to be recorded

- GARRARD LYNCH, Atto. of DEBORAH BRAMHAM, relinquished her Right of Dower of the said Land wch: is also ordered to be recorded

- Upon the Petition of ABRAHAM GOAD, ordered that RAWLEIGH DOWNE-MAN, GEORGE GLASCOCK, THOMAS GLASCOCK & DOMINICK BENNEHAM or any three of them sometime betweene this and the next Court do meet at the

House of EVE SMITH, deced., and then and there inventory and appraise the Estate of the said deced., as the same shall be presented to theire view. Capt. CHARLES BARBER is requested to administer an Oath to the Gentlemen above named for theire true inventorying of the said deced.'s Estate as also to the said ABRAHAM GOAD for the true delivery thereof

    - Judgment is granted Capt. HENRY BRERETON against ELIZABETH LYNCH, Exrx. of STEPHEN LYNCH, for six hundred and sixty seven pounds of tobbo. due by Account proved by the Oath of the Plt., wch: is ordered to be paid with costs of suite als exo

    - Mr. THOMAS THORNE entered Attorney for JOSHUA STONE

    - In the action of Trespass betweene WINIFRED GLASCOCK by her prochein amy, GEORGE GLASCOCK, Plt. and ABRAHAM GOAD, Defendt., for fifty pounds Sterl. damage by meanes of the Defendt.'s entering upon a certaine parcell or tract of land of the Plt.'s containeing two hundred and eighty acres wth: the appurtenances situate in the Parish of Farnham & County aforesd., and cutting downe, carrying away & converting to his owne use five timber trees of the Plt.'s, and for his breaking up the (   ) thereof

p.   Richmond County Court 5th of December 1705
96   and committing severall other trespasses thereon to the Plt.'s great damage &c., to which the Defendt. in his proper person came into Court and pleaded Not Guilty, and GEORGE GLASCOCK in behalfe of WINIFRED GLASCOCK praying that the land aforesd. be layed ut by a Jury, it is therefore ordered that the Sherriff of this County summons a Jury of the most able and antient freeholders of the County, inhabitants as neare as may be to the land in controversie & lyable to no just exception for affinity consanguinity or interest to meet upon the land in controversie on the fourteenth of this Instant December if faire if not the first faire day after and being first sworne before Lt. Colo. SAMUELL PEACHEY or any other Justice of the Peace for this County, are required to survey and lay out in company of Capt. CHARLES BARBER, Surveyor, the land of the Plt. according to the most antient & reputed bounds of the Patent thereof, having regard to all Patents and Evidences that shall be offered by Plt. or Defendt., and make report of theire proceedings therein to the next Court under theire hands in writing and that in case they shall find the Defendt. a Trespasser, to value the damage & report them

    - Upon the Petition of ABRAHAM DONAWAY and ELIZABETH his Wife, one of the Daughters of JOHN OVERTON, deced., for one feather bed, bolster and pillows rugg blankett sheets curtaines and valons with what did thereunto belong given unto the said ELIZA: by the Last Will and Testament of the said JOHN OVERTON, deced., Ordered that unless JOHN RANKIN and PENELOPE his Wife, Executrx. of the Last Will and Testament of the said JOHN OVERTON, do appeare att the next Court and shew cause to the contrary, that Judgment pass against the said JNO: & PENELOPE in theire qualification aforesd., for the Legacy so given to the said ELIZABETH and which the said ABRAHAM & ELIZABETH humbly pray Order for together wth: costs

    - EVAN JACOB, Servant to NATHANIEL THRIFT, being presented to this Court for inspection into his age, is adjudged thirteene yeares and ordered that he be exempted from payment of Levys till the time appointed for the same according to Act

- Upon the Petition of JONE DENIN, late Servant to THOMAS DEACUS, for her Corne and Cloathes according to Act, Capt. ALEXANDER DONIPHAN certifying to the Court that the same was due to her, Judgment is thereupon granted unto the sd. JOANE against the said THOMAS DEACUS for her Corne and Cloathes according to Act to be paid wth: costs als exo

- Upon the motion of Mr. THOMAS MACKEY, Mr. DANIELL McCARTY entered his generall Attorney

- Upon the Petition of RICHARD WHITE and SARAH his Wife, Widdow and Relict of WILLIAM HANKS, deced., agt. WILLIAM HANKS, JUNR., Admr. of the said deced., for her part or portion of the hoggs that belonged to the Estate of the said deced., they being not inserted in the Inventory of the deced.'s Estate by WILLIAM HANKS, his Admr., it is thereupon ordered that sometime betweene this and the next Court WILLIAM HANKS

p.   Richmond County Court 5th of December 1705
97   do bring a supplementary Inventory of the number of Hoggs belonging to the
        Estate of the deced. and insert the same into the Inventory thereof and that
they be divided betweene the said WILLIAM HANKS and other the Children of the deced., and that he make report of his proceedings therein to the said next Court

- Upon the Petition of JOHN BARTHOLOMEW, ordered that he be for the future exempted the payment of Levys by reason of his age and inability to labour

- Upon the Petition of THOMAS WELSH agaisnt DENNIS CAMERON & JANE his Wife, Admrx. of WALTER WELSH, the Petitioner's Father, for his part or portion of his Father's Estate now in the hands of DENNIS CAMERON. Ordered that unless the said DENNIS CAMERON and JANE his Wife appeare att the next Court & shew cause to the contrary, Judgment do pass against them in theire qualification aforesd. to THOMAS WELSH for his part or portion of his deced. Father's Estate according to the Inventory and Appraisment thereof

- The Court adjourned till Eight of the Clock in the morning

- Att a Court held for Richmond County the Sixth day of Xber Ano. 1705
                              Present

Lieut. Colo. SAMLL. PEACHEY   Capt. CHARLES BARBER
Majr. WM. ROBINSON   Capt. NICHOLAS SMITH
Capt. ALEXANDER DONIPHAN   Mr. EDWARD BARROW
Mr. JOSHUA DAVIS   Mr. JOSEPH DEEKE   Justices

- This day Lieut. Colo. GEORGE TAYLER having first taken the Oaths appointed by Act of Parliament to be taken instead of the Oathes of Allegiance and Supremacy and subscribed the Test took also the Oath for the duely executing the Office of a Justice of the Peace for this County

- MARGARETT CHISWICK, late Servant to Mr. JOSEPH BELFIELD, being presented by the Grand Jury for bareing a mulato bastard & the said MARGT. confessing the fault and acknowledging that the said Child was begott by a Negro, the Court have ordered that she be sold by the Church Wardens of Sittenburne Parish for the terme of five yeares & that the produce of the sd. Fine be disposed of for the use of the said Parish according to Act of Assembly in that case made and provided

- Mr. HENRY SEGAR makeing Oath that neither he nor any person to his knowledge had taken up the Land due unto him for importation of DANIELL MURRY RICHARD LAUGHY and KATHERINE REYLEY, Certificate is thereupon granted unto him

p.   Richmond County Court 6th of December 1705
98   for one hundred and fifty acres of Land as is usuall in such cases, the right of which he assignes in Court to Mr. EDWARD BARROW

- This day MRS. SUSANNA TAYLER came into Court and did voluntarily relinquish her Right of Dower of the Plantation and tract of land where her former Husband, ELIAS WILSON, deced., did live, to ELIAS WILSON, JUNR., the which Lieut. Colo. GEORGE TAYLER, Husband to the said SUSANNA, did acknowledge that he did consent to and the same is ordered to be recorded

- GEORGE RADFORD being taken by the Sherriff of this County upon execution against him att the suite of Mr. HENRY ASTINE and the Prison of this County being insufficient, Ordered that Capt. JNO: TARPLEY, Sherriff, do take him into his custody and that he be paid for the same att the next laying of the Levy att the rate of foure hundred pounds of tobbo. per moneth for so long as he shall keep him or till such time as GEORGE RADFORD shall comply wth: is Creditor aforesd. and that if he shall by any meanes make escape that then Capt. JNO: TARPLEY shall stand lyable for the payment of his Creditor aforesd., and also to indemnify the Court of the said County

- This day ROBERT THORNTON confest Judgment to Majr. JAMES BOUGHAN for seven hundred and thirty pounds of sweet sented tobbo and caske due upon a sealed Bill which is ordered to be paid with costs als exo

- This day ROBERT THORNTON confest Judgment to EDWARD JEFFEREYS for five hundred pounds of tobbo. due by Bill which is ordered to be paid wth: costs als exo

- This day ROBERT THORNTON confest Judgment to JAMES SHAW for seven hundred and seventy pounds of tobbo. due by Bill which is ordered to be paid with costs also exo

- This day ROBERT THORNTON confest Judgment to GARRARD LYNCH for six hundred eighty foure pounds of tobbo. due upon a Bond, which is ordered to be paid wth: costs of suite als exo

- The insufficiency of the Prison of this County being this day offered to the consideration of the Court and the great prejudice that may ensue thereon, it is therefore ordered that Lieut. Colo. GEORGE TAYLER, Majr. WM. ROBINSON and Capt. NICHOLAS SMITH or any two of them do meet att the Courthouse of this County on Tuesday next being the Eleventh instant and do then and there agree with Mr. EDWARD BARROW or any other person as they shall think capable of performing the same wth: all convenient speed for the building of a strong and sufficient Prison, a paire of Stocks and Whipping Post as also a Stable for the securing of Gentlemens' Horses that do belong to the Court

- Ordered that THOMAZIN MARSHALL be paid by RICHARD PHILLIPS for five days attendance according to Act being by him subpaened as an Evidence

p.   Richmond County Court 6th of December 1705
99   upon presentment of the Grand Jury against him for concealing a Tythable

- JAMES STEPHENSON being summoned to appeare att this Court upon presentment of the Grand Jury agt. him for not goeing to Church for six months together and failing to appeare, ordered that he be fined for the same according to Law and that he pay the same wth: costs als exo

- JAMES STEVENSON being summoned to appeare att this Court to answer unto the presentment of the Grand Jury against him for not goeing to Church for six months together and contemptuously refuseing, ordered that the Sherriff of this County do take him into custody till he shall give Bond for his appeareance att the next Court to answer for his Contempt aforesaid

- Upon the Petition of JAMES LAUGHAN that he might be admitted to erect and build a Mill on a certain run or water course in this County called SHORTS RUN and he having land on the one side of the said Run, ordered that Mr. GEORGE HEALE, JOHN SEAMAN and JEFFEREY REYNOLDS or any two of them some time betweene this and the next Court do meet at the House of JOHN SEAMAN in order to lay out and value one acre of land on the opposite side of the said Run and report the same to the next Court under theire hands in writing

- Upon the Petition of ARTHUR DYE, in behalfe of his Son, AVERY DYE, against PATIENCE NAILER, Executrx. of the Last Will and Testament of AVERY NAYLER, deced., for thirty thousand pounds of tobbo. being a Legacy given to the said AVERY DYE by the Last Will and Testament of AVERY NAYLER, the said ARTHUR DYE giving security to indemnify the Worspll her Majties Justices for this County for the repayment of the same to AVERY DYE when he shall attaine to age sufficient to demand the same; Judgment is therefore granted to ARTHUR DYE in behalfe of his Son, AVERY DYE, against PATIENCE NAYLER, Executrx. of the Last Will and Testament of AVERY NAYLER, for the summe of thirty thousand pounds of tobbo. together with costs als exo

- This day FRANCIS WILLIAMS and WILLIAM SISSON came into Court and acknowledged themselves indebted to the Worshpll. her Majties. Justices for the sd. County in the full and just summe of sixty thousand pounds of tobbo. to be paid to the Justices theire heires &c. in case ARTHUR DYE, Father of AVERY DYE, do not repay & refund to AVERY DYE when he shall attaine to sufficient age to receive the same the summe of thirty thousand pounds of tobbo. being a Legacy given to AVERY DYE by the Last Will and Testament of AVERY NAYLER, deced., and for which PATIENCE NAYLER, Exrx. of the Last Will and Testament of AVERY NAYLOR, did this day confess Judgment for to ARTHUR DYE on behalfe of the said AVERY DYE

p.   <u>Richmond County Court 6th of December 1705</u>
100   Richmond County is Dr. to the severall Claymes hereafter mentioned, vizt.

	Tobbo.
To Capt. ALEXANDER DONIPHAN	0047
To JANE CAMMELL	0800
To Capt. WILLIAM UNDERWOOD	0014
To JAMES SHERLOCK, Clk. R. C.	0800
To Colo. WILLIAM TAYLOE	1000
To Capt. CHARLES BARBER	2000
To Capt. BEALE, CRASKE, BARBER & BRERETON theire 4 companies	5653
To Mr. RANDOLPH for costs of Laws & Levy	0350
To Mr. Secretary JENNINGS	0160

To JAMES STROTHER	0440
To ELIZABETH HILL for Rumm & Sugar att Publick Thanksgiving which she assignes to Colo. GEORGE TAYLER	0900
To MRS. ELIZABETH BRADLEY, Exrx. of THOMAS BRADLEY, for his makeing a Barr & a Table for the Court	0550
To EDWARD JEFFEREYS for cleaning the Courthouse which he assignes to Colo. GEORGE TAYLER	0500
To DAVID JACKSON for cutting the Bever Dam att Monocon	0100
To THOMAS LEWIS for keeping TOTUSKEY FERRY	5000
To JAMES SHERLOCK, Clk., R. C.	1080
To Capt. JNO: TARPLEY for Rumm and Sugar att Publick Thanksgiving	1500
To Capt. JNO: TARPLEY, Sherriff, for extraordinary service	1000
To Colo. WILLIAM TAYLOE, Burgess expences and his man's	9252
To Majr. WILLIAM ROBINSON Burgess expences and his man's att two Sessions of Assembly	16027
To Capt. CHARLES BARBER, late Sherriff, for Irons for the Indian Prisoners Secretary fees & 7 Levys dead & runaway	2121
To Colo. WILLIAM TAYLOE for calling a Court	1000
To Capt. ALEXANDER DONIPHAN for one Inquest	0133
To JOHN OLDHAM for 7 Woolves heads	1400
To JOHN FENNELL one Woolfes head killed in a Pitt	0300
To GEORGE TOMLIN for one Woolfes head taken in a Pitt	0300
To HENRY BERRY for one Woolfes head	0200
To CHRISTOPHER PRITCHETT two Woolfes heads killed wth: a Gunn	0400
To JOSEPH RUSSELL for 2 Woolfes heads killed with a Gunn	0400
To the first Article of Colo. WILLIAM TAYLOE's Account	1000
To Capt. CHARLES BARBER for the trouble of his House while the Indian prisoners were there, 43 Indians, 55 days	3000
To Mr. NATHANIEL POPE for the Coppy of the Genll. Court Rules	0500
To Mr. DANLL. McCARTY and Mr. GEORGE ESKRIDGE each 1000	2000
To THOMAS DICKENSON	0500
To Sallary of 60000 att 10 p cent	6006
To Sallary of 6900 att 10 p cent	0690
	66756

p.
101   **Richmond County Court 6th of December 1705**

By severall Fines in Colo. TAYLOE's hands	1800
By WILLIAM STONE, MARTIN HAMMOND, JNO. DALTON, STEPHEN GIBBIN & WM. TRIPLETT, each 100	0500
By GEORGE PAYNE, FRANCIS WILLIAMS, FRANCIS STONE, JAMES SCOTT, JNO. WILLIS, JNO. HANSFORD, WILLIAM STROTHER, ROBERT STROTHER, BENJAMIN STROTHER, JOHN GRIMSLEY, WILLIAM MARSHALL, ISAAC ARNOLD, Jury each fined for not returning a perfect Verdict 150	1800
By THOMAS JESPER, PHILLIP HARRIS, WM. ALGOOD, WM. LAMBERT, CHARLES CALE, CHARLES STEWARD, STEPHEN FEWELL, WM. TRIPLETT, JNO: BERRY, GEORGE HOPKINS Delinqts. of Grand Jury each fined 200	2000
	6900
	66756
	59856

- The Country and County Levy for this yeare being 38 pounds & one quarter of a pound of tobbo. per poll together, ordered that Capt. JOHN TARPLEY, Sherriff of this County of his Deputy, do collect so much of every Tythable person in this County and out thereof pay to each respective Creditor of the Country or County all the summes herein contained and in case any person or person shall refuse to pay the same that then the said Capt. JOHN TARPLEY or his Deputy do make distress for the same and for his or theire so doeing this shall be theire sufficient Warrant

　　- This day JOSEPH BRAGG confest Judgment to Mr. JOSEPH DEEKE for nineteene hundred & sixteene pounds of tobbo. due by Bill which is ordered to be paid wth: costs als exo

　　- This day Capt. JNO. TARPLEY confest Judgment to the Church Wardens of Sittenburne Parish for the use of the Parish for two thousand pounds of tobbo, which is ordered to be paid wth: costs als exo

　　- This day MARGARETT CHISWICK came into Court and voluntarily did acknowledge that shee was willing to serve Capt. WILLIAM BARBER or his assignes the terme of one yeare after her time for wch: she was sold to JOHN FENNELL by the Church Wardens of Sittenburne Parish in consideration of Capt. BARBER buying her from Capt. JNO: TARPLEY, who purchased her of the said JNO: FENNELL

　　- Upon consideration of the first Article of Colo. WILLIAM TAYLOE's Accot. the Court being divided in theire opinion concerning the same, it is continued till next Court

　　- Upon consideration of the last Article of Colo. WILLIAM TAYLOE's Accot. the Court have thought fitt to continue the same till next Court for want of the Order made att the Court called att the House of Colo. WILLIAM TAYLOE

p.　　Richmond County Court 6th of December 1705
102　　intrusting him wth: the NANZATICO INDIANS

PHILLIP HARRIS	THOMAS JESPER	WILLIAM ALGOOD
WILLIAM LAMBERT	CHARLES CALE	CHARLES STEWARD
STEPHEN HOWELL	WILLIAM TRIPLETT	JNO. BERRY &
GEORGE HOPKINS		

failing to give in their presentments with the rest of the Grand Jury it is therefore ordered that they be severally fined according to Act

　　- The Court adjourned till tomorrow Eight of the Clock

　　- Att a Court held for Richmond County the 7th day of Xber 1705
　　　　　　　　　　　Present

Lieut. Colo. GEORGE TAYLER	Mr. EDWARD BARROW	
Majr. WM. ROBINSON	Mr. NICHO: SMITH	Justices
Capt. ALEXANDER DONIPHAN	Mr. JOSEPH DEEKE	
Mr. JOSHUA DAVIS		

　　- Upon the motion of Mr. JOSHUA DAVIS, ordered that the Deposition sworne to by SAMLL. BAYLY relateing to the matter in difference betweene the sd. JOSHUA DAVIS, Plt. and RICHARD TALIAFERRO, Defendt. be recorded

　　- In the action of Trespass betweene JOHN WHITE and MARGT. his Wife, Plts. and JOHN SYMMONS, Defendt., ordered that Capt. CHARLES BARBER, late Sherrif of this County, be summoned to appeare att the next Court to shew cause why he do not returne the report of the Jury in the said suite

　　- The Petition preferred by JOB HAMMOND, JUNR. Guardian & Tutor of KATHERINE, MERCY & THOMAS BAYLIS, Children of THOMAS BAYLIS, the

Elder, deced., against JAMES SUGGITT is dismist, the Plt. saying it was done
    - The Attachment granted to SEM COX against the Estate of JAMES
PHILLIPS is continued att the Defendt.'s charge till next Court
    - The action of Debt betweene JOHN FORSTER, Plt. and GEORGE PHIL-
LIPS, Defendt., for nine hundred pounds of tobbo. due by Bill, the Defendt. appeareing
and saying that he had drawne a Note payable to the Defendt. on JAMES STOTT of
LANCASTER County for the summe of nine hundred pounds of tobbo. wch: is not
yett returned. Upon consideration whereof the Court have ordered that if GEORGE
PHILLIPS shall att the next Court produce a Certificate from any Justice of the
Peace before whome JAMES STOTT shall depose and make Oath that he hath paid
the contents or any part of the aforesd. Note so drawne upon him by GEORGE
PHILLIPS that in such case so much shall be allowed as discount to GEORGE
PHILLIPS, otherwise that Judgment pass against him for the summe of nine hun-
dred pounds of tobbo. according to Declaration together with costs of suite als exo.

p.   Richmond County Court 7th of December 1705
103   - The action brought by JOHN WORDEN against JAMES STOREY is continued till next Court
    - Judgment upon Attachment is granted to PETER EVANS against the
Estate of DANIEL BURGES for sixty pounds of tobbo. and six ells of dowlass
attached in ye hands of BARTHOLOMEW DAWSEY, which is ordered to be paid wth:
costs als exo
    - The Bill in Chancery exhibited by JOHN TARPLEY, Father and prochein
amy of JOHN TARPLEY, JUNR., against CHRISTOPHER ROBINSON & JUDITH
his Wife, THOMAS GRIFFIN and PETER PRESSLEY and WINIFRED his Wife,
Exrx. of the Last Will and Testament of CORBIN GRIFFIN, deced., is dismist, one of
the Executors aforesaid being since deceased
    - In an action of Case betweene PETER EVANS, Plt. and EDWARD BAR-
ROW, Defendt., for six hundred and sixty foure pounds of tobbo. due by Accot., the
Defendt. appeareing and praying that it might be continued for the evidence of Doctor
JOHN WORDEN, the Court had ordered that unless the said JOHN WORDEN
appeare att the next Court and give his evidence in behalfe of EDWARD BARROW
relateing to the matter in dispute, that then EDWARD BARROW plead over and
come to tryall wth: the said Plt. EVANS
    - In the action of Debt betweene WILLIAM THORNTON, Plt. and JAMES
PHILLIPS, Defendt., for thirteene hundred and fifty two pounds of sweet sented
tobbo. due by Bill, the Defendt. being returned by the Sherriff by a Copy left and
failing to appeare, Attachment is therefore granted to the Plt. for the said summe
against the Estate of the Defendt. returnable to the next Court for Judgment
    - In an action of Debt between ALEXANDER DONIPHAN, Plt. and LAW-
RENCE YOUNG, Defendt., for eight hundred and eighty two pounds of tobbo., the
Defendt. being returned by the Sherriff non est inventus and failing to appeare,
Attachment is therefore granted to the Plt. for the summe aforesaid against the
Estate of LAWRENCE YOUNG returnable to the next Court for Judgment
    - The action brought by MARK RYMER against JOHN WISE is dismist, the
Plt. not prosecuting
    - In an action of Debt betweene JOHN LOMAX, Plt. and JEREMIAH
STROTHER, Defendt., for six hundred pounds of tobbo. and caske due by Bill dated

8 ber 21st 1703, the Defendt. by GEORGE ESKRIDGE his Attorney came into Court and for Pleas saith that true it is that the Defednt. did at the instance of the Plt. pass the Bill aforesd. in consideration of Rent for the Plantation where the Defendt. then lived att which time the Plt. by writeing under his hand which date is the same with the Bill aforesd. did oblidge himselfe his heires &c. to secure and indemnifye the Defendt. what Rents he should pay him for the Plantation aforesd. as by the said obligation relation thereto had may more fully and att large appeare. Nevertheless one GAWEN CORBIN, Esqr., since the makeing of the Bill and Writing aforesd. hath made distress of the tobbaccoes of this Defendt. for the Rent of the Plantation wherefore as much as the Plt. hath not secured and held indemnifyed the Defendt. according to his Obligation, this Defendt. prays Judgmt. if the Plt. aforesd. agt. this Defendt. his action aforesd. ought to have and maintaine, and the Plt. by DANLL. McCARTY his Attorney for Replication saith that notwithstanding anything by the Defendt. alledged he from his action ought not to be barred for that, tho true it is yt. he gave the Defendt. such obligation as he alledged yett the Plt. saith that the Defendt. hath never yett suffered any inconveniency or damage for any Rents paid by him to the

p.   Richmond County Court 7th of December 1795
104   Plt. and the Plt. saith that according to the contents of his said obligation, he
       now and always was ready to save harmless and indemnifye the Defendt. without that GAWIN CORBIN, Esqr., never made any legall distress on the tobbaccoe of the Defendt. and this he is ready to verifie and prayed Judgmt. according to Declaration, which being read & heard and the Defendt. praying till another Court to rejoyne, the Court having had - - - - - consideration thereon are of opinion that it ought not to be allowed for that the said action had beene continued two severall Courts and therefore grant Judgmt. against JEREMIAH STROTHER to JOHN LOMAX for the summe of six hundred pounds of tobbo. and caske, wch: is ordered to be paid wth: costs of suite als exo.
       From which Judgment the said JEREMIAH STROTHER appeales to the Sixth day of the next Generall Court for a reheareing
       - This day WILLIAM MARSHALL and JOB HAMMOND acknowledged themselves indebted unto JOHN LOMAX in the summe of two thousand pounds of tobbo. to be paid to JNO. LOMAX in case JEREMIAH STROTHER do not prosecute an appeale by him made from a Judgmt. of this Court this day obtained against him by JOHN LOMAX to the Sixth day of the next Generall Court
       - In an action of Debt betweene STEPHEN SEBSATIN, Plt. and ANTHO. SEALE, Defendt, for thirty good Buck Skins and twelve good Doe Skins due by Bill, the Defendt. being returned by the Sherriff non est inventus and not appeareing, Attachment is therefore granted the Plt. against the Estate of the Defendt. for the number of skinns aforesaid returnable to the next Court for Judgment
       - In an action of Debt betweene STEVEN SEBASTIN, Plt. and ANTHO. SEALE, Defendt., for thirty good Buck Skins and ten good Doe Skins and ten pounds Sterl. damage, the Defendt. being returned by the Sherriff non est inventus and not appeareing, Attachment is therefore granted to the Plt. against the Estate of the Defendt. for the number of Skinns and damage aforesaid returnable to the next Court for Judgment
       - The action brought by PATIENCE NAYLER, Exrx. of the Last Will and Tes-

tament of AVERY NAYLER, deced. agt. JOSEPH BELFIELD is dismist, the Plt. not prosecuting

- The action brought by Majr. WILLIAM ROBINSON against NEHEMIAH JONES is continued till next Court

- Judgment is granted to THOMAS WHITE against THOMAS DEACUS for five hundred and thirteene pounds of tobbo. due by Bill, which is ordered to be paid wth: costs of suite als exo

- This day the Last Will and Testament of CHRISTOPHER JONES being presented to this Court for proofe, the same was proved by the Oath of Capt. NICHOLAS SMITH and the Probate thereof continued till next Court for the evidence of ELIZA: ELAM, the other wittness to the said Will

- In an action of the Case betweene JOSEPH TAYLOE, Plt. and CHARLES DODSON, JUNR., Defendt. for three thousand two hundred pounds of tobbo. damage as in the Plt.'s Declaraton is sett forth by meanes of the Defendt.'s not warranting unto

p.   Richmond County Court 7th of December 1705
105   the said JOSEPH one black gelding according to his promise and assumption laid downe in the Plt.'s Declaration, wch: black gelding is since taken by due course of Law so that thereby the Plt. hath no remedy. Judgment being granted last Court against CHARLES BARBER, late Sherriff for the said summe unless the Defendt. should appeare att this Court to answer the said action, and the Defendt. failing to appeare, it is therefore ordered that CHARLES BARBER, late Sherrif of this County, pay unto the said JOSEPH TAYLOE the said summe of three thousand two hundred pounds of tobbo. together wth: costs of suite als exo

- Upon the motion of Capt. CHARLES BARBER, late Sherriff of this County, ordered that the Attachment granted to him last Court against the Estate of CHARLES DODSON, JUNR. for the summe of three thousand two hundred pounds of tobbo. damage for the non appeareance said CHARLES DODSON att the suite of Colo. WILLIAM TAYLOE be continued till next Court returnable for Judgmt.

- In an action of Trespass betweene WILLIAM BARBER and JOYCE his Wife, Plts. and SAMLL. SAMFORD, of ye Parish of Northfarnham & County of Richmond, Planter, for one hundred pounds Sterl., damage by meanes of the Defendt. entering upon a certaine tract or parcell of land of the Plt.'s situate & being in the Parish of Farnham in County of Richmond containeing two thousand three hundred acres and cutting downe carrying away and converting to his owne use forty timber trees that grew thereon & committing severall other trespasses to the Plt.'s great damage &c.,

To which the Defendt. by WILLIAM DARE, his Attorney, comes into Court and pleads Not Guilty,

Whereupon the Court have ordered that the Sherrif of this County do summons a Jury of the most able and antient freeholders of the Vicinage, inhabitants as neare as may be to the land in controversie and lyable to no just exception by affinity, consanguinity or interest, to meet upon the land aforesaid on the first Wednesday in Janry. next if faire, if not on the next faire day after, and being first sworne before Mr. SAMLL. PEACHEY or any other Justice of the Peace for the sd. County, having regard for all Patents and Evidences to survey and lay out the land of the Plt. according to the most antient and reputed bounds of the Patent thereof, and to make report of theire proceedings therein to the next Court and that in case they do find the Defendt. a Trespasser, to value the damages and report them

- The action brought by ELIZABETH WOODWARD, Admrx. of all and singular the goods & chattles of WILLIAM WOODWARD, deced., against CORMACK McKENNY, is dismist, the Plt. not prosecuting

- This day SAMLL. GODWIN, Attorney of JOSEPH RUSSELL, confest Judgment to KATHERINE GWYN, Exrx. of Majr. DAVIS GWYN for seven hundred and forty pounds of sweet sented tobbaccoe due by Bill, wch: is ordered to be paid wth: costs of suite als exo.

- JOHN MINNIFY makeing Oath that neither nor any person to his knowledge had taken up the Land due to him for the importation of JNO: MINNIFY and MARGT. MENING, Certificate is thereupon granted unto him for one hundred acres of land as is usuall in such cases, the right of which he assignes in Court to Mr. JOSHUA DAVIS

- Nonsuite is granted to THOMAS FINWICK agaisnt EDWARD JEFFEREYS for the insufficiency of the Plt.'s Declaration which is ordered to be paid wth: costs of suite als exo.

p.   Richmond County Court 7th of December 1705
106   - WILLIAM SMITH being subpaened as an Evidence for THOMAS FINWICK in a suite betweene him and EDWARD JEFFEREYS & therein having attended four days, ordered that WILLIAM SMITH be paid by THOMAS FINWICK for the same according to Law als exo

- The action brought by ANDREW SAULSBURY against PETER EVANS is dismist, the Plt. not prosecuting

- The action brought by PETER EVANS against ANDREW SAULSBURY is dismist, the Plt. not prosecuting

- The action brought by EDWARD NEWTON against DANLL. McGWYRE is continued by the consent of both parties

- The action brought by ROBERT PAYNE against ABRAHAM HANNASON is dismist, the Plt. not prosecuting

- The action brought by ROBERT PAYNE against ABRAHAM HANNASON is dismist, the Plt. not prosecuting

- The Attachment granted last Court to ROBERT PAYNE against the Estate of DANIELL MERRITT is continued till next Court

- The action brought by SYMON PASCOE against THOMAS HARPER is continued till next Court

- In an action of Case betweene EDWARD JONES, Plt. and JOHN BROWNE, Defendt. for one thousand pounds of toobo. damage, upon breach of a certaine agreement betweene the Plt. and Defendt., the Defendt. faileing to appeare to answer the same, the Judgmt. of the last Court is therefore confirmed to the Plt. against MARTIN HAMMOND, the security returned for the Defendt.'s appeareance, for the summe of foure hundred and twenty five pounds of tobbo., being the ballance of the Plt.'s Account being proved by him upon Oath and it is ordered that he pay the same to the Plt. with costs als exo

- The action brought by JAMES CAWARD agt. GEORGE BLEWFORD is dismist, the Plt. not prosecuting

- In an action of Debt betweene ROBERT CLARKE, Plt. and JOHN DALTON and MARY his Wife, Defendts. for five hundred and thirty foure pounds of tobbo. and three shillings in money due by Bill under the hand of the said MARY, who when sole, the Plt. makeing Oath tht the said JOHN DALTON did assume upon himselfe the payment of the said Bill. Judgment is therefore granted to the Plt. against the Defendts. for the summe of five hundred and thirty foure pounds of tobbo. & three shillings in money, and it is ordered that he pay the same wth: costs als exo

   - In an action of Debt betweene WILLIM HANKS, Admr. of WILLIAM HANKS, deced., & HENRY JENNINGS, Defendt., the Plt. faileing to appeare and prosecute the same, it is therefore ordered that he be nonsuited and pay the Defendt. damages according to Law and costs als exo

   - The action brought by WILLIAM HANKS, Admr. of WILLIAM HANKS, deced., against JAMES PEARSON is dismist, the Plt. not prosecuting

   - The action brought by ALEXANDER CAMBELL against HENRY JENINGS is dismist, the Plt. not prosecuting

p.   Richmond County Court 7th of December 1705
107   - The Ejectione Firma brought by WILLIAM BARBER against THOMAS GLASCOCK is continued till next Court

   - The action brought by Doctor ROBERT CLARKE against SAMLL. SAMFORD, Exexutr. of JAMES SAMFORD, is continued till next Court by consent of the Plt.

   - Judgment is granted to MARY BURK against ROBERT KING for foure hundred and fifty pounds of tobbo. due by Bill, which is ordered to be paid wth: costs of suite als exo

   - The action brought by JOSHUA DAVIS against RICHARD TALIAFERRO is continued till next Court

   - The Ejectione Firma brought by DOMINICK BENNEHAN agt. ROWLAND LAWSON is continued till next Court

   - In an action of Detinue betweene JOHN KELLY, Plt. and JAMES TRENT, Defendt., for three thousand pounds of tobbo. damage by meanes of the Defendt. detaineing from the Plt. one bay stone Horse branted wth: a flower de luce, the Defendt. in his proper person came into Court and for Plea did say that he doth not detaine any Horse of JOHN KELLY and for tryall therof putts himselfe upon the Country, and the Plt. likewise. Whereupon a Jury was impannelled and sworne to try the matter att issue by name

JOSEPH BELFIELD	JAMES INGO	JNO: DALTON
WM. SIMONS	THO: PETTY	WM. SMITH, Tanner
WM. JENKINS	WM. MARSHALL	WM. YATES
JOB HAMMOND	ANDREW DEW and	WM. PANNELL

who being returned brought in for Verdict; We of the Jury do find for the Plt. fifty pounds of tobbo. damage and his Horse to be delivered; which Verdict upon the motion of GEORGE ESKRIDGE, Attorney for the Plt., is ordered to be recorded and Judgmt. ganted to the Plt. agt. JAMES TRENT for the summe of fifty pounds of tobo & the present delivery of the Horse aforesd. together with costs of suite als exo

   - In an action of Debt betweene ROBERT GIBSON and RUTH his Wife, JOSEPH BELFIELD and FRANCES his Wife, Admrx. of the goods and chattles of MOTREM WRIGHT, deced,, Plts. and CHARLES DODSON, JUNR., Defendt. for foure hundred and fifteene pounds of tobbo. due on ballance of a Bill, the Defendt. faileing to appeare to answer the same, the Judgment of the last Court is therefore confirmed to the Plt. against JOSHUA STONE, Security returned for the Defendt.'s appeareance, for the said summe of foure hundred and fifteene pounds of tobbo., and it is ordered that he pay the same to the Plt. with costs als exo

 - THOMAS BECK, Servant to WILLIAM PANNELL, being presented to this Court for inspection into his age is adjudged eleven yeares old and ordered that he be exempted from payment of Levys till time appointed for the same according to Act

 - In an action of Debt betweene THOMAS GRIFFIN, Plt. and JOHN BROWNE, Defendt., for six hundred and fourty five pounds of tobbo. due by Bill, Judgment being granted the last Court against the Sherriff for the said summe unless the Defendt. should appeare att this Court to answer the said action; and the Defendt. faileing to appeare, it is therefore ordered that Capt. JOHN TARPLEY, Sherriff of this County, do pay unto THOMAS GRIFFIN the summe of six hundred and fourty five pounds of tobbo. wth: costs als exo

p. Richmond County Court 7th of December 1705
108 - The Attachment granted last Court to the Sherriff against the Estate of
  JOHN BROWNE for the summe of six hundred and fourty five pounds of tobbo. is continued till next Court returnable for Judgmt.

 - The Attachment granted last Court to GAWEN CORBIN agt. the Estate of JOSEPH LEWRIGHT for seven hundred pounds of tobbo. and caske due by Bill, the Defendt. not appeareing is continued returnable to the next Court for Judgment

 - The action brought by THOMAS GRIFFIN against WILLIAM MARSHALL is dismist, the Plt. not prosecuting

 - The action brought by THOMAS GRIFFIN against JOHN SETTLE is dismist the Plt. not prosecuting

 - JOHN BOWEN hath order granted for five days attendance according to Law agt. JOHN KELLY as an evidence in the suite betweene him and JAMES TRENT, to be paid wth: costs als exo

 - JAMES WILSON hath order granted for five days attendance according to Law against JOHN KELLY as an evidence in the suite betweene him and JAMES TRENT to be paid wth: costs als exo

 - Judgment is granted to JOSEPH BELFIELD against PATRICK TIFFY for six hundred and seventy pounds of tobbo. due by Accot. proved by the Oath of the Plt., which is ordered to be paid wth: costs of suite als exo

 - Ordered that WILLIAM RENNELLS do keep a PUBLIC FERRY over RAPPA: RIVER to the most convenient Landing on the other side the River and that he be paid for the same at the laying of the Levy the summe of two thousand foure hundred pounds of tobbo. as is usuall

 - Ordered that THOMAS LEWIS do continue keeping TOTUSKEY FERRY & that he be paid for the same att the next laying of the Levy as is usuall

 - Ordered that THOMAS LEWIS do keep ORDINARY att his Dwelling House and that he give Bond for the same according to Act

 - Ordered that JOHN WILLIS, JUNR. be Surveyor of the Highwayes for the ensueing yeare in the precincts betweene UNDERWOOD's MILL & the DOEG SWAMP

 - Ordered that JNO. ARMSTRONG be Surveyor of the Highwayes for the

ensueing yeare in the precincts betweene LAMBS CREEKE & the head of the River
    - Ordered that THOMAS WHITE be Surveyor of the Highwayes for the
ensueing yeare in the precincts betweene DOEG SWAMP & LAMBS CREEKE
    - The Citation commenced by HUGH FRENCH, one of the Sons of HUGH
FRENCH, late of this County, deced., by WILLIAM TRIPLETT his prochein amy
against JOHN SUMERVELL and MARGT., his Wife, Exrx. of the Last Will and
Testament of HUGH FRENCH, deced., is dismist, the Plt. not prosecuting
    - The presentment of the Grand Jury against JAMES WILSON of Farnham
Parish for concealeing a Tythable is dismist, the person thought to be concealed not
cohabiting wth: him att that time

p.   Richmond County Court 7th of December 1705
109   - The presentment of the Grand Jury against EDWARD JEFFEREYS,
        Ordinary Keeper, for sweareing three Oaths is dismist
    - The presentment of the Grand Jury against EDWARD JEFFEREYS for not
selling Drink in lawfull measures is dismist, nothing appeareing to the contrary
    - The Court adjourned till the first Wednesday in February next

    - Att a Court held for Richmond County the 6th day of February 1705
                     Present her Majties Justices
Colo. WILLIAM TAYLOE   Majr. WILLIAM ROBINSON
Lieut. Colo. GEORGE TAYLER   Mr. JOSHUA DAVIS   Justices
Lieut. Col. SAMLL. PEACHEY

    - Upon the Petiton of ANNE OLDHAM, Order for Admon. is granted to her on
all and singular the Estate of JOHN OLDHAM, deced., shee giveing security according to Law
    - This day PHILLIP HARRIS acknowledged himself indebted to the Worspll.
her Majties Justices for Richmond County in the full and just summe of twenty thousand pounds of tobbo. to be paid to the said Justices their heires Exrs. and Admrs. in
case ANNE OLDHAM, Widdo. of JOHN OLDHAM, deced., do not duely administer on
all and singular the Estate of the said deced., and render a true Account thereof when
thereunto lawfully called
    - And whereas upon reading the Orders, the Court having received Credible
information that the Estate of the above named JOHN OLDHAM, deced., would
amount to more then the assumpsitt or security given, it is thereupon ordered that no
admon. be granted till further security be given for the same
    - Upon the Petition of Majr. WILLIAM ROBINSON that he might be admitted
to erect and build a Mill on a certaine Runn or water course in this County called
PAYNES RUNN, and he having land onely on the one side thereof, Ordered that Mr.
JOHN BIRKETT, FRANCIS STONE and WM. PANNELL sometime betweene this
and the next Court do meet att the House of Majr. WILLIAM ROBINSON in order to
lay out and value and acre of land on the opposite side of the said Runn and make report of theire proceedings to the next Court under theire hands in writing
    - This day, JAMES PHILLIPS acknowledged a Deed for Land to Collo. WM.
FITZHUGH wch: is ordered to be recorded

p.   Richmond County Court 6th of February 1705/1706
110   - This day the Last Will and Testament of CHARLES DODSON, deced.,
        being presented to this Court by the Executrx. therein named for proofe, the
same was proved by the Oath of CHRISTOPHER PATTY, who came into Court and
made Oath that he had read the sd. Will, and that the said CHARLES DODSON,
deced., in his lifetime did declare to him that that was his Last Will and the Probate
thereof is continued till next Court
        - This day the Last Will and Testament of GEORGE TOMLIN, deced., being
presented to this Court by the Exrx. therein named for proofe, the same was proved
by the Oaths of JAMES INGO, SARAH LILLY & HENRY STREET and order for
Probate granted thereon
        - This day the Last Will and Testament of JOHN McMILLION being pre-
sented to this Court by the Executrx. therein named for proofe, the same was proved
by the Oaths of JOHN FENNELL and HENRY STREET and order for Probate
granted thereon
        - This day the Nuncupative Will of ALEXANDER PITTENDRICK being pre-
sented to this Court by Mr. JOHN CHARTRES for proofe, the same was proved by
the oaths of Colo. WILLIAM TAYLOE and RICHARD SERJANT and by the affir-
mation according to Statute of DANIELL FOSSETT and order for Probate granted
thereon
        - This day the Inventory of EVE SMITH's Estate being presented to this
Court by Mr. GEORGE GLASCOCK, the same is ordered to be recorded
        - Ordered that WILLIAM WOODBRIDGE, GEORGE GLASCOCK, THO-
MAS DEW and ANDREW DEW, do meet att the House of JOHN OLDHAM, deced.,
sometime betweene this and the next Court and do then and there inventory and
appraise all and singular the Estate of the said deced., as the same shall be presented
to theire view. Capt. CHARLES BARBER is requested to administer an Oath to the
Appraisers for theire true appraisment of the said deced.'s Estate as also to the
Admrx. for her true delivery thereof, and make report of theire proceedings therein to
the next Court under theire hands in writing
        - This day THOMAS DEW acknowledged a Deed for Land to ANDREW DEW
wch: is ordered to be recorded
        - This day the Last Will and Testament of Doctor ROBERT CLARKE being pre-
sented to this Court by ROBERT CLARKE for proofe, the same was proved by the
Oaths of Capt. CHARLES BARBER, WILLIAM SIMMS and

p.   Richmond County Court 6th of February 1705/1706
111   AMY SIMMS, wittnesses thereto, and order for Probate granted thereon
        - This day CHARLES DODSON acknowledged a Deed for Land to CHRISTO-
PHER PATTY which is ordered to be recorded
        - Upon the Petition of CHRISTOPHER PETTY that he might be admitted to
erect and build a Mill on a certaine Runn or water course in this County called by the
name RUNN of TOTUSKEY and he having land onely on one side of the said Runn,
ordered that PETER ELMORE, THOMAS DODSON and CHARLES DODSON do
meet att the House of CHRISTOPHER PETTY and do lay out and value an acre of
land on the opposite side of the said Runn and make report of theire proceedings
therein to the next Court under theire hands in writing
        - THOMAS THORNE is entered Attorney for THOMAS LLOYD

    - Upon the Petition of MOOTA, an East India Indian belonging to Capt. THOMAS BEALE, surviving Executr. of Mr. WILLIAM COLSTON, deced., for his Freedome, ordered that the said Capt. THOMAS BEALE be summoned to appeare att the next Court to shew Cause if any he can why the said MOOTA should not be free

    - Upon the Petition of SEMBO, an East India Indian, Servant to JNO: LLOYD Esqr., for his freedome, ordered that Mr. GRIFFIN FAUNTLEROY, Atto. of the said JOHN LLOYD, Esqr., be summoned to appeare att the next Court and shew cause if any he can why the said SEMBO should not be free

    - This day JOHN DAVIS acknowledged an Assignment of a Deed for Land to JAMES KITCHEN wch: is ordered to be recorded

    - This day JAMES KITCHEN and ELIZABETH his wife acknowledged a Deed for Land to RICHARD HILL wch: is ordered to be recorded, and the said ELIZABETH being examined, did voluntarily declare that shee did the same wth:out any manner of constraint or compulsion thereto, wch: is ordered to be recorded

    - This day JOHN CHAMP acknowledged a Deed for Land to THOMAS BATCHELOR wch: is ordered to be recorded

    - This day SAMLL. WALTON acknowledged a Deed for Land & Assignment thereof endorsed wth: Bond to HENRY LONG wch: is ordered to be recorded

    - This day CHRISTOPHER PRIDHAM acknowledged a Deed for Land to DAVID BERRICK, wch: is ordered to be recorded

    - MARY PRIDHAM, Wife of CHRISTOPHER, relinquished her Right of Dower to the said Land, which is ordered to be recorded

p.   <u>Richmond County Court 6th of February 1705/1706</u>
112   - Upon the Petition of JANE WATTSON, Order for Admon. is granted her on
        all and singular the Estate of WILLIAM WATTSON, deced., shee giving
security according to Law

    - This day EDWARD MOZINGO and DAVID McGUIRE acknowledged themselves indebted unto the Worpll. her Majties Justices for the County of Richmond in the full and just summe of twenty thousand pounds of tobbo. to be paid to the said Justices theire heires Exrs. and Admrs. in case JANE WATTSON do not duely administer on all and singular the Estate of WILLIAM WATTSON, deced., and render a true Account thereof when thereunto lawfully called

    - Ordered that JOHN FENNELL, JNO: FENNELL, JUNR., JAMES INGO, EDWARD NEWTON and RICHARD CLIFTON or any three or more of them some time betweene this and the next Court inventory and appraise all and singular the Estate of WILLIAM WATTSON, deceased, and make report of theire proceedings therein to the next Court under theire hands in writing. Lt. Colo. GEO. TAYLER is requested to administer an Oath to ye Appraisers for their true appraisment of the sd. deced.'s Estate and also to the Admrx. for her true delivery thereof

    - Upon the Petition of ELIZABETH TRAVERS, one of the Daughters and Surviving Executrix. of the Last Will and Testament of SAMLL. TRAVERS, late of this County, Gent., deceased, setting forth that the said SAMLL. TRAVERS did by his Last Will and Testament in writing duely proved in this Court (inter alia) nominate constitute ordaine and appoint his then Wife, the aforesaid ELIZABETH, and his Brother, RAWLEIGH, Exrs. thereof, and that soone after the death of the said SAMLL. the aforesaid Testator's aforesd. Wife departed this life, and the aforesd.

ELIZABETH being then a Minor and not capable to performe the Office of Exrx., the aforesd. RAWLEIGH entered into the execution thereof and thereby became possest of all and singular the Estate of the said SAMLL., and sometime after the said RAW-LEIGH being so possest made his Last Will and Testament & appointed Capt. THO-MAS BEALE and Mr. JOHN TAVERNER, Executrs. thereof, and dyed, wch: said Executrs. proved said Will and accepted the Executorship & by virtue thereof possest themselves of all and singular the goods and chattles rights and creditts of Wares & Merchandize of the said SAMUELL, deceased, and that they the sd. Exrs. the Estate of the aforesd. SAMLL. or any part thereof to the aforesd. ELIZABETH who is onely surviving Exrx. of the Last Will and Testament of the aforesaid SAMUELL, deced., ever have and still do refuse and deny praying that the said Capt. THOMAS BEALE and Mr. JOHN TAVERNER, Exrs. as aforesd. might be summoned to shew cause if any they could why they rendered not to the said ELIZABETH the Estate as aforesd. the Estate of the aforesd. SAMLL. TRAVERS according to the purport

p.   Richmond County Court 6th of February 1705/1706
113   of her said Petition. The said Capt. THOMAS BEALE and Mr. JOHN
        TAVERNER, Exrs. as aforesd., appeareing and offerring nothing in barr thereof, it is therefore ordered that Colo. SAMLL. PEACHEY, Capt. CHARLES BARBER, Mr. WILLIAM WOODBRIDGE, Mr. SAMLL. SAMFORD and Mr. EDWARD JONES or any three or more of them do meet at the House of the said SAMLL. TRAVERS, deced., on the twenty fifth day of this instant February and do then and there lay out and separate the Estate of the said SAMUEL TRAVERS from the Estate of the said RAWLEIGH TRAVERS in quantity quality and such specie (as neare as may be) as the same was att the time it was appraised by them, ye sd. WILLIAM WOODBRIDGE, SAMLL. SAMFORD and EDWARD JONES, And the said Colo. SAMUELL PEACHEY, Capt. CHARLES BARBER, WILLIAM WOOD-BRIDGE, SAMUELL SAMFORD and EDWARD JONES are further ordered and required to inspect and audit the Accounts of the said RAWLEIGH TRAVERS and to make report of theire whole proceedings to the said next Court under their hands in writing

        - This day FRANCIS SLAUGHTER having first taken the Oath appointed by Act of Parliamt. to be taken instead of the Oathes of Allegiance and Supremacy and subscribed the Test, tooke also the Oaths of a Justice of the peace for this County

        - This day GARRARD LYNCH came into Court and made Oath tht the severall articles contained in the Account exhibitted by Capt. CHARLES BARBER, were expended upon the Account of the Publick att the Court of Oyer & Terminer for the tryall of the Indians

        - This day Colo. WILLIAM TAYLOE, having first taken Oaths appointed by Act of Parliament to be taken instead of the Oathes of Allegiance and Supremacy and subscribed the Test tooke also the Oth of a Justice of the Peace for the said County

        - This day EDWARD JEFFEREYS came into Court and made Oath that the severall particulars contained in the Account exhibitted by him against Capt. CHARLES BARBER were delivered to such persons as said they came by the Sherriff's order

        - This day THOMAS BURK confessed Judgment to Mr. ANTHONY LYNCH for one thousand and foure hundred pounds of sweet sented tobbo. and caske due by Bill, which is ordered to be paid wth: costs of suite als exo.

- Upon the motion of Capt. CHARLES BARBER, it is ordered tht he is hereby impowered to make distress for any Publick Dues remaineing unpaid of his last yeare's Accounts

p.   Richmond County Court 6th of Februry 1705/1706
114   - Mr. DANIELL McCARTY and Mr. GEORGE ESKRIDGE entered Attorneys for Capt. CHARLES BARBER
       - The Order made last Court for WILLIAM HANKS to returne a supplementary Inventory of the hoggs belonging to the Estate of WILLIAM HANKS, deced., continued and ordered that he returne the same to the next Court
       - The Order to summon JAMES STEPHENSON upon presentment of the Grand Jury against him for not goeing to Church for six months together and for his Contempt in refuseing to appeare att this Court pursuant to the last Court's Order, continued till next Court
       - The Order for JAMES LAUGHAN to returne the Appraismt. of Land to build a Mill continued till next Court
       - The Probate of the Last Will and Testament of CHRISTOPHER JONES, continued till next Court for the evidence of ELIZABETH ELAM
       - In an action of Trespass betweene WINIFRED GLASCOCK by GEORGE GLASCOCK her prochein amy, Plt., and ABRAHAM GOAD, Defendt., for fifty pounds Sterl. damage by meanes of the Defendt.'s committing divers trespasses upon a certaine tract or parcell of land of the Plt.'s containeing two hundred & eighty acres of land scituate lying & being in the Parish of Farnham and County of Richmond, the Defendt. appeareing att the last Court and pleading Not Guilty & a Survey wth: a Jury on the fourteenth day of December last, if faire if not the next faire day after thereupon ordered wch: being not complyed with according to the tenour of the said Order, upon the motion of the Plt. by Mr. DANIELL McCARTY, her Atto., the same is continued, and it is ordered that the Sherriff of this County summon a Jury of the most able and antient freeholders of the County, inhabitants as neare as may be to the land in controversie and lyable to no just exception by affinity consanguinity or interest to meet on the 18th instant if faire if not on the next faire day after on the land in controversie and being first sworne before Lieut Colo. SAMLL. PEACHEY or any other Justice of the Peace for the sd. County, having regard to all Patents and Evidences offered by Plt. and Defendt., are required to survey and lay out in company of Capt. CHARLES BARBER, Surveyor, the land of the Plt. according to the most antient and reputed bounds thereof and to make report of theire proceedings therein to the next Court under theire hands in writing & in case they do find the Defendt. a Trespasser to value the damages & report them

p.   Richmond County Court 6th of February 1705/170
115   - The Petition of ABRAHAM DONAWAY & ELIZA: his Wife against JOHN RANKIN and PENELOPE his Wife, Exrx. of the Last Will and Testament of JOHN OVERTON, deced., is dismist, neither party appeareing
       - The Petition of THOMAS WELSH against DENNIS CAMERON and JANE his Wife, Admrx. of WALTER WELSH, deced., is dismist, neither party appeareing
       - Mr. DANLL: McCARTY and GEORGE ESKRIDGE entered Attornies for ALEXANDER FLEMING

- The Court is adjourned till tomorrow morning Eight p Clock

- Att a Court held for Richmond County the 7th day of February 1705
Present

Colo. WILLIAM TAYLOE   Capt. NICHO: SMITH
Lieut. Colo. SAMLL. PEACHEY   Mr. EDWARD BARROW   Justices
Majr. WILLIAM ROBINSON   Mr. FRANCIS SLAUGHTER
Mr. JOSHUA DAVIS

- In an action of Trespass betweene JOHN WHITE and MARGARET his Wife Plts., and JOHN SIMMONS, Defendt., for fifty pounds Sterl., damage by meanes of the Defendt.'s committing diver trespasses upon a certaine tract or parcell of land of the Plts. containeing three hundred and fifty acres scituate lying and being in the Parish of Farnham in County of Richmond as in the Plts's Declaration is expressed. A Survey with a Jury according to an Order of Court of the Eighth day of March last past (and then continued by severall continuances till now) being made, and it appeareing by the report thereof this day returned that the Jury have found severall trespasses committed by the Defendt., & five shillings Sterl., damage. The Defendt. by his Atto., DANLL. McCARTY, appeared and said tht the said Verdict was not rightly returned and the Court having heard the severall arguments insisted upon by the Plts. and Defendt., are of opinion tht the Verdict is good and well returned, and upon the motion of the Plts. by GEO: ESKRIDGE, theire Attorney, it is ordered to be recorded, And it is thereupon considered adjudged & ordered that the Defendt. pay unto the Plts. the said summe of five shillings Sterl. and costs als exo
From which Judgment the Defendt. appeales to the 6th day of the next Generall Court for a reheareing

p.   Richmond County Court 7th of February 1705/1706
116   - This day GEORGE GLASCOCK acknowledged himselfe indebted to JOHN
       WHITE and MARGARET his Wife in the full and just summe of one hundred pounds Sterl., to be paid to the said JOHN & MARGT., theire heires Exrs. and Admrs. in case JOHN SYMONS do not prosecute an appeale by him made from an Order of Court this day obtained agt. him in an action of Trespass wherein JOHN WHITE and MARGT. his Wife are Plts. and JOHN SIMONS Defendt.
       - ALEXANDER SPENCE makeing Oath that neither he nor any person to his knowledge had taken up the land due to him for the importation of JAMES NAUGHTY, HONORIA SHELANE, LYDIA ARMFIELD, KATHERINE JONES, SUSANNA REDWOOD, SUSANNA WOOLDRIDGE, JAMES FLANNIGIN, SARAH JONES, Certificate is thereupon granted unto him for foure hundred acres of land as is usuall in such cases the right of which in Court he assignes to Mr. JOSHUA DAVIS
       - GYLES MATHEWS makeing Oath that neither he nor any person to his knowledge had taken up the land due to him for the importation of RICHARD CLAX-TON, THOMAS POTTS, WILLIAM SMITH, ROBERT McNEAR, MARGERY KELLY, HANNA DEALY, JOHN BAKER & JANE MARTIN; Certificate is thereupon granted to him for foure hundred acres of land as is usuall in such cases, the right of which he assignes in Court to Mr. JOSHUA DAVIS
       - WILLIAM LAMBERT makeing Oath that neither he nor any person to his

knowledge had taken up the land due unto him for the importation of JOSEPH
PARISH, RICHARD CROSS, ELIZABETH WOOD, ANNE TOOL, JOSEPH
TAYLER & HENRY BRINBLE. Certificate is thereupon granted to him for three
hundred acres of land as is usuall in such cases, the right of wch: he assignes in Court
to Mr. JOSHUA DAVIS
          - Nonsuite is granted to JAMES PHILLIPS against SEM COX, there being no
cause of action and it is ordered that he pay the same to the said JAMES wth: costs
als exo
          - In an action of Case betweene SEM COX, Plt. and JAMES PHILLIPS,
Defendt., the Defendt. makeing Oath to an Account exhibitted by him against the
Account of the Plt., wch: did ballance, it is thereupon ordered that the said SEM COX
be nonsuited and that he pay the same to the said JAMES PHILLIPS wth: costs als
exo
          - In an action of Debt betweene JOHN FORSTER, Plt. and GEORGE PHIL-
LIPS, Defendt. for nine hundred pounds of tobbo. due by Bill, JNO: STOTT appeareing and makeing Oath that he had allowed so much to the sd.

p.   Richmond County Court 7th of February 1705/1706
117   JOHN FORSTER on Account of the said GEORGE PHILLIPS, it is therefore
          ordered that the sd. JOHN FORSTER be nonsuited and that he pay the same
to GEORGE PHILLIPS wth: costs als exo
          - The action brought by JOHN WORDEN against JAMES STORY is dismist,
the Plt. not prosecuting
          - In an action of Debt betweene WILLIAM THORNTON, Plt., and JAMES
PHILLIPS, Defendt. for thirteene hundred and fifty two pounds of tobbo. due by Bill,
the Defendt. appeareing and makeing Oath tht he had paid the summe of seven hundred and seventy pounds of tobbo. in part of the said Bill, Judgment is thereupon
granted to WILLIAM THORNTON for five hundred and eighty two pounds of tobbo,
the ballance of the sd. Bill and itt is ordered that the sd. Defendt. pay the same wth:
costs als exo.
          - The action brought by PETER EVANS against EDWARD BARROW is dis-
mist, the Plt. not prosecuting
          - In an action of Debt betweene STEPHEN SEBASTIN, Plt. and ANTHO.
SEALE, Defendt., for thirty good Buckskins and twelve good Doe skins due by Bill, the
Defendt. being to the last Court returned non est inventus & Attachment thereon
issued and this day returned by the Sherriff (nulla bona) upon the motion of the Plt.
Attachment is renewed unto him agt. the Estate of ANTHONY SEALE for the num-
ber of skins aforesaid returnable to the next Court for Judgmt.
          - In an action of Debt betweene STEPHEN SEBASTIN, Plt. and ANTHONY
SEALE, Defendt., for thirty good Buckskins and ten good Doe skins and ten pounds
Sterl. damage, the Defendt. being returned by the Sherriff to the last Court non est
inventus and an Attachment thereupon issued, and this day returned nulla bona,
Upon the motion of the Plt., Attachment is renewed unto him agt. the Estate of the
Defendt. for the number of skins and damage aforesaid returnable to the next Court
for Judgment
          - Judgment is granted to Majr. WILLIAM ROBINSON against NEHEMIAH
JONES for twelve pounds, ten shillings & one penny halfe penny due by Accot.
proved by the Oath of the Plt. wch: is ordered to be paid with costs of suite als exo

- In an action of Trespass betweene WILLIAM CLARKE and JOYCE his Wife Plts., and SAMLL. SAMFORD, Planter of the Parish of Northfarnham and County of Richmond, Defendt., for one hundred pounds Sterl. damage by meanes of the Defendt. committing diver trespasses on one certaine

p.   Richmond County Court 7th of February 1705/1706
118   tract or parcell of land of the Plts. containeing two thousand three hundred
          acres scituate lying and being in the Parish and County aforesaid neare
TOTUSKEY CREEKE, as in the Declaration is expressed; the said Defendt., by
WILLIAM DAIRE, his Atto., appeareing att the last Court and pleading Not Guilty
and a survey with a Jury on the first Wednesday in January last past if faire if not
the next faire day after thereupon ordered to be, wch; being not complyed with according to the tenor of the aforesaid Order, upon the motion of the Plt. by his Atto.,
GEORGE ESKRIDGE, it is ordered that the Sherrif of the County do summon a Jury
of the most able and antient freeholders of the Vicinage inhabitants as neare as may
be to the land in controversie and lyable to no just exceptions by affinity consanguinity or interest to meet on the twenty second day of this instant February if faire if not
the next faire day after upon the land of the Plts. and being first sworne before Lt.
Colo. SAMLL. PEACHEY or any other Justices of the peace for the sd. County are
required in company with Capt. CHARLES SMITH, Surveyor (haveing regard to all
Patents and Evidences offered by Plts. or Defendt.) to survey and lay out the same
according to the most antient and reputed bounds of the Patent thereof and to make
report of theire proceedings therein to the next Court under theire hands in writing
and that in case they shall find the Defendt. a Trespasser, to value the same & report
them
          - Judgment is granted EDWARD NEWTON against DANIELL McGWYRE
for foure hundred and fifty pounds of tobbo. wch: is ordered to be paid with costs of
suite als exo
          - The action brought by ROBERT PAYNE against DANIELL MERRITT is
dismist, the Plt. not prosecuting
          - Judgment is granted to SYMON PASCOE against THOMAS HARPER for
six hundred and twenty six pounds of tobbo. due upon ballance of an Account, wch: is
ordered to be paid wth: costs of suite als exo
          - The Ejectione Firma depending in this Court betweene WILLIAM BARBER,
Plt. and THOMAS GLASCOCK, Defendt., is continued till next Court
          - The action brought by ROBERT CLARKE agt. SAMLL. SAMFORD, Exr. of
JAMES SAMFORD, is dismist, the Plt. being dead
          - The action brought by JOSHUA DAVIS against RICHARD TALIAFERRO
is dismist, the Plt. not prosecuting

p.   Richmond County Court 7th of February 1705/1706
119   - The Ejectione Firma depending in this Court betweene DOMINICK
          BENNEHAN, Plt. and ROWLAND LAWSON, Defendt. for the Defendt.
ousting the Plt. from a certaine plantation with the appurtenances scitaute lying and
being in the Parish of Farnham and County of Richmond containeing three hundred
acres and now or late in the possession of WILLIAM DOWNEMAN, wch: JOHN
SHARP of LANCASTER County did demise to the said DOMINICK for a terme of
yeares not yett expired. Mr. GEORGE GLASCOCK makeing Oath that he had

served WILLIAM DOWNEMAN, Tenant in possession of the lands and premises aforesaid wth: a copy of the Plt.'s Declaration in this behalfe and the notice thereon endorsed, ordered that unless the said WM. DOWNEMAN or those under whome he claymes do appeare att the next Court (having had due notice of this Order by the Sherriff of this County or his Deputy) and confess Lease Entry & Ouster & insist only on the Tryall of the Title, Judgment pass against him by default

- In the action of Debt brought by GAWEN CORBIN, Plt. agt. JOSEPH LEWRIGHT, Defendt., for seven hundred pounds of tobbo. and caske, Attachment being issued upon the last Court's Order against the Estate of the Defendt. for the summe aforesaid, and this day returned (nulla bona), Upon the motion of the Plt., the same is renewed unto him for the sume aforesd. agt. the Estate of the Defendt. returnable to the next Court for Judgment

- The action brought by THOMAS GRIFFIN agt. JOHN BROWNE is dismist, the Plt. not prosecting

- The Attachment granted last Court to the Sherriff against the Estate of CHARLES DODSON, JUNR., is dismist, no presentation

- This day GARRARD LYNCH made Oath that the particulars contained in the Account exhibited by Capt. CHARLES BARBER (this entry does not seem complete)

- The action brought by Doctor ROBERT CLARKE against WILLIAM AL-GOOD is dismist, the Plt. not prosecuting

- In an action of Debt betweene ANNE FLYNT, Plt. and RODERICK JONES, Defendt. for one thousand pounds of tobbo. due upon Bond, the Defendt. being returned by the Sherriff by copy left and fayling to appeare, on the motion of the Plt. Attachment is granted her against the Estate of the Defendt. for the said summe returnable to the next Court for Judgmt.

- Especiall Imparlance is granted in the suite betweene ALEXANDER FLEMING, Plt. and SAMLL. SAMFORD, Defendt. till next Court

- The action brought by JOSEPH TAYLOE agt. ALEXANDER LIGHTON is dismist, the Plt. not prosecuting

- The action brought by JOSEPH TAYLOE vs. ROBERT HUGHES is dismist, no prosecution

p.   Richmond County Court 7th of February 1795/1706
120   - This day ALEXANDER SPENCE confest Judgment to JOB HAMMOND
      for one thousand pounds of tobbo. due upon Bill and Account, wch: is ordered to be paid with costs of suite als exo

- The action brought by Capt. WILLIAM FOX against JOHN TANTER is dismist, the Plt. not prosecuting

- The action brought by RICHARD HUGHES, Assignee of JOHN LAWRENCE, against TIMOTHY CANADY is dismist, the Plt. not prosecuting

- The action brought by JOHN HUGHES, Assignee of JOHN LAWRENCE, against TIMOTHY CANNADY is dismist, ye Plt. not prosecuting

- In an action of Debt between EDWARD JONES, Plt. and SAMLL. BAYLY, Defendt. for nine hundred and seven pounds of tobbo. due upon ballance of an Accot., the Defendt. being called and not appeareing nor any security returned, Judgment is therefore granted to the Plt. agt. the Sherriff for the summe aforesaid unless the Defendt. appeare att the next Court and answer the said action

- Judgment being this day past against the Sherriff for nine hundred and seven pounds of tobbo.unto EDWARD JONES for the non appeareance of SAMLL. BAYLY att the suite of said EDWARD, upon the motion of the Sherriff, Attachment is granted him agt. the Estate of SAMLL. BAYLY for the summe of nine hundred and seven pounds of tobbo. returnable to the next Court for Judgmt.

- The action brought by SARAH RADFORD agaisnt RANDALL DOUGLAS is dismist, the Plt. not prosecuting
- The action brought by JAMES LAUGHAN agt. ANDREW SAULSBURY is dismist, the Plt. not prosecuting
- The action brought by GARRARD LYNCH agt. THOMAS LOYD is dismist, the Plt. not prosecuting
- The actin brought by WILLIAM PANNELL agt. GARRARD LYNCH is dismist, the Plt. not prosecuting
- The action brought by JOSEPH DEEKE agt. WALTER WRIGHT is dismist, the Plt. not prosecuting
- The action brought by THOMAS LOYD agt. JAMES BIDDLECOMB is dismist, the Plt. not prosecuting
- The action brought by JOHN GALLOFER agt. JOHN FITZGERALD is dismist, the Plt. not prosecuting
- The action brought by JOSEPH BRAGG agt. ANNE GREENE, Admrx. of RICHARD GREENE, is dismist, the Plt. not prosecuting

p.   Richmond County Court 7th of February 1705/1706
121   - The action brought by GEORGE THOMPSON against THOMAS HUGHES
       is dismist, the Plt. not prosecuting
- The action brought by WEBLEY PAVEY against THOMAS SMITH is dismist the Plt. not prosecuting
- The action brought by JOHN POUND against JOHN LANE is dismist, the Plt. not prosecuting
- The action brought by WILLIAM JENKINS against SAMLL. CHURCHILL is dismist, the Plt. not prosecuting
- In the action of Debt betweene THOMAS MACKEY, Plt. and JOSHUA STONE, Defendt., for thirty three pounds, eight shillings and nine pence upon a Protested Bill of Exchange as in the Plt.'s Declaration is expressed, the Defendt. by his Attorney, THOMAS THORNE, came into Court and for Plea saith non est factum. Upon the motion by DANLL. McCARTY, his Atto., time is given him till next Court to reply or demurr
- The action brought by JOHN LANE against JOSEPH DEEKE is dismist, the Plt. not prosecuting
- The action brought by JOSEPH DEEKE against JOHN LANE is dismist, the Plt. not prosecuting
- The action brought by GARRARD LYNCH agt. ROBERT THORNTON is dismist, the Plt. not prosecuting
- The action brought by Ralph (? MARR) agt. JOHN FITZGERALD is dismist, the Plt. not prosecuting
- The action brought by EDWARD BRYAN against JOHN GALLOFER is dismist, the Plt. not prosecuting
- The action brought by Capt. WILLIAM FOX against JOAN LOVETT is dismist, the Plt. not prosecuting

- The action brought by PHOEBE SLAUGHTER agt. THOMAS MERRI-
WETHER is dismist, the Plt. not prosecuting

- In an action of Case betweene KATHERINE GWYN, Exrx. of the Last Will
and Testament of Majr. DAVID GWYN, Plt. and SAMLL. BAYLY, Defendt., for five
pounds, five shillings & three pence Sterl. due by Accot., the Defendt. being called and
not appeareing nor any security returned, Judgment is therefore granted to the Plt.
agt. the Sherriff for the said summe unless the Defendt. appeare att the next Court
and answer the said action

- Judgment being this day past against the Sherriff for five pounds, five shillings & three pence Sterl. unto KATHERINE GWYN, Exrx. of the Last Will and Testament of Majr. DAVID GWYN, for the non appeareance of SAMUELL BAYLY att
the suit of the said KATHERINE

p.   Richmond County Court 7th of February 1705/1706
122   Upon the motion of the Sherriff an Attachment is granted him against the
        Estate of SAMLL. BAYLY for the summe aforesaid returnable to the next
Court for Judgment

- The action brought by JAMES NAVID against MICHAEL CONNER is dismist, the Plt. not prosecuting

- Ordered that the Sherriff do aquaint Mr. GYLES WEBB that there is a new
Commission of the Peace for this County whereon he is appointed one of the Justices
and that he summon him to the next Court to be sworne according to the directions of
the Dedimus for administering the Oath and Test to the Justices of the Peace for the
said County

- Upon the Petition of JANE THODY, Order for Admon. is granted unto her on
all and singular the Estate of RICHARD THODY she giving security according to
Law

- This day JOB HAMMOND and RICHARD WISDELL acknowledged them-
selves indebted unto the Worspll. her Majties Justices for Richmond County in the full
and just summe of twenty thousand pounds of tobbo. to be paid to the Justices theire
Exrs. or Admrs. in case JANE THODY do not duely administer on all and singular the
Estate of RICHARD THODY, deceased, and render a true Account thereof when
thereunto lawfully called

- Ordered that Mr. MOORE FANTLEROY, EDWARD BRYAN, DAVID
LEWIS, THOMAS WILLIAMS and THOMAS WARD or any three or more of them
sometime betweene this and the next Court do meet att the House of Madm.
KATHERINE GWYN and do then and there inventory and appraise all and singular
the Estate of RICHARD THODY, deced., as the same shall be presented to theire
view, and make report of theire proceedings threin to the next Court under theire
hands in writing. Collo. WILLIAM TAYLOE is requested to administer an Oath to the
Appraisers for theire true appraisment of the said deced.'s Estate as also to the
Admrx. for the true delivery thereof

- Especiall Imparlance is granted in the suite betweene JOHN DALTON, Plt.
and ELIZABETH LYNCH, Admrx. of STEPHEN LYNCH, deced., Defendt. till next
Court

- In an action of Case betweene JOHN DALTON and MARY his Wife, Admrx.
of WILLIAM BROCKENBROUGH, deced., Plts. and JOHN MILLS, JUNR. Executr.
of JAMES GILBERT, deced., Defendt. for three hundred and thirty foure

p.   Richmond County Court 7th of February 1705/1706

123   pounds of tobbo., the Defendt being returned by the Sherriff by Copy left and not appeareing, upon the motion of the Plt. an Attachment is granted unto him against the Estate of the Defendt. for the summe aforesaid returnable to the next Court for Judgment

- In an action of Case betweene JOHN DALTON, Plt. and SAMLL. BAYLY, Defendt., for eleven hundred and twenty one pounds of tobbo. upon ballance of Accots. the Defendt. being called and not appeareing nor any security returned, Judgment is therefore granted to the Plt. against the Sheriff for the summe aforesd. unless the Defendt. appeare att the next Court and answer the said action

- Judgment being this day past against the Sherriff for eleven hundred and twenty one pounds of tobbo. unto JOHN DALTON for the non appeareance of SAMLL. BAYLY att the suite of the said JOHN, upon the motion of the Sherriff an Attachment is granted him agt. the Estate of SAMLL. BAYLY for the summe aforesaid returnable to the next Court for Judgment

- Nonsuite is granted to EDWARD JEFFEREYS for the non appeareance of JOHN SOMERVALL, wch: is ordered to be paid wth: costs als exo

- The action brought by Capt. JOHN TARPLEY agt. THOMAS JENKINS is dismsit, the Plt. not prosecuting

- The action brought by RALPH BARTLETT agt. RICHARD APPLEBY is dismist, the Plt. not prosecuting

- Especiall Imparlance is granted in the suite betweene WILLIAM SMITH, Tanner, Plt. and ALEXANDER SINKLER, Defendt. till next Court

- The action of Case brought by JOHN DALTON and MARY his Wife, Admrx. of WILLIAM BROCKENBROUGH deced., agt. JOSHUA DAVIS is continued till next Court by consent

- The action brought by CHARLES SNEAD agt. THOMAS PATTY is dismist, the Plt. not prosecuting

- The action of EDWARD JONES against JOHN DALTON as marrying MARY, the Widdo. & Admrx. of WILLIAM BROCKENBROUGH, deced., is dismist, the Plt. not prosecuting

- The action brought by JOHN DALTON and MARY his Wife, Admrx. of WILLIAM BROCKENBROUGH, deced., agt. EDWARD JONES is dismist, the Plts. not prosecuting

- The action brought by EDWARD ROCH against MARK RYMER, JUNR. is dismist, the Plt. not prosecuting

- The action brought by JAMES KITCHEN agt. RICHARD WASHBURNE is dismist, the Plt. not prosecuting

p.   Richmond County Court 7th of February 1705/1706

124   - The action brought by EDWARD JEFFEREYS against JOSHUA DAVIS is dismist, the Plt. not prosecuting

- The suite in Chancery commenced by HUGH FRENCH by WILLIAM TRIPLETT his Guardian and prochein amy agt. JOHN SOMERVELL and MARGARET his Wife, late MARGT. FRENCH, Exrx. of the Last Will and Testament of HUGH FRENCH, deced., is dismist, the Plt. not prosecuting

- The action brought by JAMES SUGGITT agt. CHRISTOPHER PRITCHETT is dismist, the Plt. not prosecuting

- The action brought by THOMAS GLOVER against SAMLL. SHORT is dismist the Plt. not prosecuting
- The action brought by KATHERINE GWYN, Exrx. of the Last Will and Testament of Majr. DAVID GWYN, deced., agt. GEORGE RADFORD is dismist, the Plt. not prosecuting
- The action brought agt. JAMES NELSON by GEORGE RADFORD is dismist, the Plt. not prosecuting
- The action brought by JOHN WISE agt. MARGARET RYMER is dismist, the Plt. not prosecuting
- Especiall Imparlance is granted in the suite betweene WILLIAM SMITH, Tanner, Plt. and WILLIAM YATES, Defendt., till next Court
- The action brought by WILLIAM COMBS and MARY his wife agt. WILLIAM PITTMAN is dismist, the Plts. not prosecuting
- The action brought by MARY RICHARDSON, Admrx. of the goods & chattles of JOHN RICHARDSON, deced., v. ANDREW BAKER is dismist, the Plt. not prosecuting
- The action of Case brought by MARY RICHARDSON, Admrx. of the goods & chattles of JOHN RICHARDSON, deced., agt. ANDREW BAKER is dismist, the Plt. not prosecuting
- The action brought by JUSTIN STEELE agt. BENJAMIN MOSELY is dismist, the Plt. not prosecuting
- The action brought by JOSEPH BELFIELD against DANIEL McGWYRE is dismist, the Plt. not prosecuting
- Especiall Imparlance is granted in the suite betweene WILLIAM YATES, Plt. and WILLIAM SMITH, Tanner, Defendt., till next Court
- The action brought by FRANCIS STONE against JOSEPH WOODWARD is dismist, the Plt. not prosecuting
- The action brought by JOHN MINIFY agt. JOHN PALMER is dismist, the Plt. not prosecuting

p.   Richmond County Court 7th of February 1705/1706
125   - The action brought by WILLIAM SMITH, Tanner, agt. JOHN MINIFY is
       dismist, the Plt. not prosecuting
- The action brought by JOHN MINIFY and MARGARET his Wife agt. WILLIAM SMITH, Tanner, is dismist, the Plts. not prosecuting
- In an action of Trespass betweene ALEXANDER SPENCE and ELIZA-BETH his Wife, Plts. and WILLIAM HAMMETT, Defendt., the Plts. not appeareing to prosecute the same, upon the motion of the Defendt. it is ordered that they be nonsuited and that they pay the same to the Defendt. and costa als exo
- Refference is granted in the suite between WILLIAM HAMMETT & SARAH his Wife, Plts. and ALEXANDER SPENCE, Defendt., till next Court
- In an action of Case between ALEXANDER SPENCE, Plt. and WILLIAM HAMMETT, Defendt., the Plt. not appeareing to prosecute the same, it is therefore ordered that he be nonsuited and that he pay the same to the Defendt. and costs als exo.
- In an action of Trespass betweene ALEXANDER SPENCE, Plt. and WILLIAM HAMMETT, Defendt., the Plt. not appeareing to prosecute the same, upon the motion of the Defendt., it is ordered that he be nonsuited and that he pay the same to

the Defendt. and costs als exo.

    - The Justices's Attachment obtained by JAMES NELSON agt. the Estate of GEORGE RADFORD, neither party appeareing is dismist

    - Upon an Attachment obtained by ALEXANDER CAMBELL agt. the Estate of WILLIAM PANNELL, for eight hundred and sixty pounds of tobbo. due by Account returnable to this Court for Judgment, the same being this day returned executed upon a Mare of the Defendt.'s valued att six hundred pounds of tobbo., Judgment is thereupon granted to the Plt. agt. the Estate of the Defendt. for the summe of six hundred pounds of tobbo. als exo.

    - The action brought by FRANCIS JAMES agt. WILLIAM COOMBS is dismist, the Plt. not prosecuting

    - The action brought by FRANCIS JAMES agt. HENRY JOHN NEWEMBERG is dismist, the Plt. not prosecuting

    - The action brought by ALEXANDER SINKLER agt. WILLIAM SMITH, Tanner, is dismist, the Plt. not prosecuting

    - The action brought by WILLIAM WOODFORD, Assignee of GARRARD LYNCH, agt. JNO: MINIFY is dismist, the Plt. not prosecuting

    - The action brought by WILLIAM WILKS agt. WILLIAM COOMBS is dismist the Plt. not prosecuting

    - The action brought by EDWARD JEFFEREYS agt. ROBERT THORNTON is dismist, the Plt. not prosecuting.

    (The Richmond County Court for the 7th of February 1705/1706 continues for a number of pages. This Court will be continued in another Antient Press publication beginning on page 125 with the Court of the 7th of February 1705/1706 in the Richmond County Order Book No. 4, 1704-1708.)

AKERS.
　William 68,
ALGOOD.
　William 52, 79, 80, 95,
ALLOWAY.
　Gabriell 52,
　John 11,
　John (an Admr. of John Howell) 23,
ALMORE.
　Peter (presented -14),
AMOND.
　Joseph 44,
APPLEBY.
　Richard 18, 98,
ARMFIELD.
　Lydia 92,
ARMSTRONG.
　John 86,
ARNOLD.
　Isaac 79,
ASHBURY.
　John 11,
ASTINE.
　Anne (Wife of Henry) 53),
　Henry 42, 47, 53, 58, 60, 63, 77,

BAKER.
　Andrew (fined -35), 42, 99,
　Anne (Dau. in Law of John Baker) 10,
　John 10, 92,
BALLARD.
　William 24,
BANNEWELL.
　Robert 41,
BARBADOES.
　70,
BARBER.
　Charles Capt. (County Sheriff) 9, 10, 20, 24,
　　　　31, 43, (see Justices -52), 52, 53, 59, 63,
　　　　73, 75, 78-80, 83, 88, 90, 91, 95,
　Joyce (Wife of Wm.) 23, 52, 53, 64, 83,
　William 8, 15, 23, 52, (Capt.-54), 64, 68, 80,
　　　　83, 85, 94,
BARLOW.
　Robert 71,
BARROW.
　Edward 11-13, 16-18, (presented -47), 60, 73,
　　　　(Justice -74), 74, 77, 81, 93,
BARTHOLOMEW.
　John 76,
BARTLETT.
　Ralph 98,
BATCHELOR
　Thomas 89,
BATTAILE.
　John 62, 65,

BAYLIS.
　Katherine (Dau. of Tho., deced) 37, 56, 80,
　Mercy (Dau. of Tho., deced) 37, 56, 80,
　Thomas (deced) 19, 37, 56, 80,
　Thomas (Son of Tho., deced) 37, 56, 80,
BAYLY.
　Samuel 2, 5, 6. 12, 16, 20, 24, 33, 38, 52, 59,
　　　　80, 95-98,
BEALE.
　Joseph 33,
　Thomas (Capt.) 2, 10, 25, (see Justices -30),
　　　　37, 61, 78, 89, 90,
BECK.
　Thomas (Servt. to Wm. Pannell) 86,
BELFIELD.
　Frances (Wife of Joseph, Admrx. of Motron
　　　　Wright) 70, 85,
　Joseph 47, 62, 63, 65, 66, 70, 72, 73, 76, 83,
　　　　85, 86, 99,
BENNEHAN,
　Dominick 2, 33, 45, 70, 74, 85, 94,
　Henry 1,
BENNETT.
　Peter 72,
BENT.
　Robert 60,
BENTLY.
　Richard 54,
BERDOCK.
　Sarah 16,
BERRICK.
　David 61, 89,
BERRY.
　Henry 79,
　John 52, 79, 80,
BERWICK.
　David 2, 4, 8, 40, 41,
BEWFORD.
　George 8, 17,
BIDDLECOMB.
　James 47, 72, 96,
BIRKETT.
　John 5, 20, 87,
BLEWFORD.
　George 67, 84,
BOILE.
　James 46,
BOUGHAN.
　James Majr. 77,
BOURNE.
　James 60,
BOWEN.
　John 40, 58, 67, 71,86,
　Stephen 40, 41,
BOWLIN.
　William 7, 21,

FAUNTLEROY.
  Griffin 49, 89,
  Moore 97,
  William (deced) 10,
FENNELL.
  John 79, 80, 88, 89,
  John Junr. 89,
FENNER.
  Anne (Dau. of John) 44,
  Frances (Wife of John) 44,
  John 44, 47, 73,
FERRELL.
  Thomas 30,
FERRY -
  Public over Rappa. River 86,
  Totuskey 24, 25, 79, 86,
FEWELL.
  Stephen 79,
FINWICK.
  Thomas 65, 84,
FISHER.
  Martin 22, 52, 55,
FITZGERALD.
  John 96,
  Maurice 41,
FITZHERBERT.
  William 15, 16, 21,
FITZHUGH.
  William Colo. 87,
FLANAGAN.
  Anthony 11,
  James 92,
FLEMING.
  Alexander 58-60, 67, 91, 95,
FLETCHER.
  Joyce 51,
FLYNT.
  Anne 95,
FORELAND.
  George 42, 60,
FORSTER.
  Elinor 51,
  John 39, 40, 81, 93,
FOSSAKER.
  John (apptd. Constable -44), 57,
FOSSETT.
  Daniel 88,
FOWLER.
  Richard 15, 19,
FOX,
  Judith 70,
  Lawrence 41, 50, 70,
  Richard 7, 9,
  William Capt. 95, 96,

FRENCH.
  Hugh (Son of Hugh, deced) 53, 72, 87, 98,
  Hugh (deced) 53, 72, 87,
  Margaret (Exrx. of Hugh, now Wife of John
      Somervill) 53, 98,
FRESHWATER.
  Thomas 16,
FRISTOE.
  Robert 59,

GALLOFER.
  John 96,
GEOFFEREY.
  Edward 55,
  Thomas 55,
GIBBINS.
  James 59,
  Patrick 11,
  Stephen 79,
GIBSON.
  Robert 70, 85,
  Ruth (Wife of Robert) 70, 85,
GILBERT.
  James (deced) 4, 97,
  Mary 59,
  Mary (Exrs. of James, deced) 4,
GLADMAN.
  Thomas 6, 22, 38,
GLASCOCK.
  George 2, 13, 16, 17, 21, 25, 33, 37, 41, 43.
      52, 58, 74, 75, 88, 91, 92, 94,
  Million (Wife of George) 52,
  Thomas 68, 74, 94,
  Winefred 17, 37, 41, 43, 58, 75, 91,
GLOVER.
  Thomas 22, 38, 99,
GLOW.
  John 9,
  William (deced)(Inv. retd.-9),
GOAD / GOURD
  Abraham 15, 30, 33, 34, 41, 43, 58, 74, 75,
      91,
GODWIN.
  Samuel 53, 64, 84,
GORDEN.
  William 17,
GOULDMAN.
  Edward 42,
GOWER.
  John 40, 42, 57,
  Stanley 4, 51.
GRAHAM.
  James 7, 21,
GRAND JURY PRESENTMENTS for
  Being Drunk on Sabbath Day 14, 15, 29, 30,
  Burying a bastard Child privately 15, 30, 33,

GRAND JURY PRESENTMENTS for (contd.)
  Carrying a Gun up and down the Road on the
        Sabbath Day 14,
  Carrying a Gun in the woods on Sabbath Day
        14, 26, 29, 36,
  Committing sin of fornication and having
        bastard child 1, 3, 15, 32, 33, 36,
  Drinking & makeing merry on Sabbath Day
        14, 26, 30, 36,
  Fishing on the Sabbath Day 14, 28, 30, 35,
  Goeing to bed together as man & wife 1, 20,
  Goeing on Sabbath day to look for Deer Skins
        13, 26,
  Hanging tobacco on Sabbath Day 1,
  Hunting on Sabbath Day 29,
  Keeping company and having three Children
        13, 26, 34,
  Keeping company and having bastard Child
        13,
  Keeping company with Wife of another man
        13, 26.34,
  Not cleareing the Highwayes 15,
  Not goeing to Church for two months 14, 26,
        27, 35,
  Runaway Servants 3,
  Selling Drink on Sabbath Day 1,
  Selling Sider on Sabbath Day 29,
  Selling Rum & Sugar on Sabbath Day 14, 28,
  Speaking blasphemy 1,
  Travelling on the Sabbath day 13, 26,
  Turning out & tending Seconds 28, 35,
GRANT.
  William (presented -14), (fined -29),
GREENE.
  Anne (Admrx. of Richard) 57, 96,
  George 52,
  John 23, 39, 62,
  John Capt. 49,
  Richard 2, (presented -14), (fined -28), (Inv.
        retd. -74),
  Richard (deced) 57, 61, 96,
GREGSON.
  Thomas Capt. 16, 23,
GRIFFIN.
  Corbin (of Middlesex Co., deced) 13, 37, 81,
  Leroy (of Rappahannock Co.) 10,
  Mary 16,
  Samuel 15,
  Thomas 13, 15, 59, 71, 81, 86, 95,
GRIFFIS.
  Lewis 66,
GRIMSLEY.
  John 58, 67, 72, 79,
  Thomas 66, 72,
GROFFY.
  Mary 13,

GUBTON.
  Stephen (presented -14), 25, (fined -27),
GUY.
  George (Servant to Peter Kippax) 56,
GWYN.
  David 9,
  David Major (deced) 10, 25, 34, (Will proved
        -36), 37, (Inv. retd. -49), 62, 65, 69, 84,
        97, 99,
  Katherine Madam (former Wife of Wm. Fauntl-
        leroy, Widow of Majr. David Gwynn) 10,
        25, 34, 35, 37, 46, 47, 62, 65, 69, 84,
        97, 99,

HALE.
  George 61,
HALL.
  Robert 12,
  William (Servant to Peter Kippax -56),
HAMLETT.
  Maurice 23,
HAMMETT.
  Sarah (Wife of Wm.) 99,
  William 99,
HAMMOND.
  Amadine (Wife of Job, Junr. Admrx. of
        Thomas Baylis) 19,
  Job 9, 37, 48, 49, 52, 64, 82, 85, 95, 97,
  Job Junr. 19, 52, 58, 67,
  Job Junr. (Gdn. to Katherine, Mercy &
        Thomas Baylis) 37, 56, 80,
  Martin 79, 84,
HANCOCK.
  John (presented -14), (fined -27),
HANKS.
  Sarah 45,
  William 33, 55, 85, 91,
  William (Son of Wm., deced) 30, 33, 67, 68,
  William (deced) 30, 33, (Inv. retd. -45), 67,
        68, (Inv. retd. -74), 76, 85, 91,
  William Junr. 74, 76,
HANNASON
  Abraham (presented -14), 28, 29, 35, (former-
        ly of Maryland -36), (presentment dis-
        mist -45), 66, 84,
HANSFORD.
  John 79,
HARKIN.
  Cornelius 14, (presented -14), 26, (fined -28),
        44,
HARPER.
  George 38,
  John 2, 43, 70,
  John (Admr. of Wm.) 34,
  Thomas 19, 64, 66, 84, 94,
  William (deced) 34,

HARRIS.
  John 13, 24, (apptd. Constable -44),
  Phillip (presented -14), 24, (fined -27), 52, 79,
       80, 87,
HARRISON.
  Andrew (presented -14), 19, 28, 35, 42,
  Anne 11,
HARWOOD.
  William 18, 22, 39,
HAWKINS.
  John 22,
HAWKSFORD.
  John 5,
HAWS.
  Henry 5,
HAYES
  Henry 23, 39,
HAYWARD.
  Hugh 8,
  John 60,
HEALE.
  George 2, 78,
HENDERKIN.
  Katherine 5, 8, 20, 70,
HICKS.
  Thomas 11,
HIGGINS.
  John 8,
HIGHTOWER.
  Joshua 9, 37,
HILL.
  Elizabeth Mrs. 79,
  Richard (Ordinary Keeper)(presented -1), 89,
  William (presented -14) (fined -30, 35),
HINSON.
  Alexander (Gdn. of John Jenings) 48,
  Alexander (Gdn. of Anne Jenings) 49,
HOGAN.
  Morgan 11,
HOLMES.
  Robert 13,
HOOKE.
  Jeremiah 40, 42, 60, 62,
HOPKINS.
  George 47, 52, 79, 80,
  Robert 46,
HORE.
  Joseph 12,
HORNEBY.
  Daniel 65,
  Daniel (deced., Will proved -52), 61, (Inv.
       retd.-74),
HOWELL.
  Elizabeth 23,
  John (deced) 23,
  Stephen 52, 80,

HUCISON.
  Stephen 32,
HUGHES.
  John 95,
  Richard 95,
  Robert 95,
  Thomas 70, 96,
HUSLEAD.
  Christopher 13,

ICK.
  Timothy (Servant to James Scott) 33, 44, 49,
       51,
  William 51,
IKEY.
  John 58, 63,
INDIANS.
  Nanzatico 30-32, 49, 50, 80,
INGO.
  James 6, 8, 15, 16, 19, 21, 24, 25, 40, 42, 47,
       48, 50, 52, 53, 57, 74, 85, 88, 89,
  John 15, 16, 21, 32, 36, 40, 41, 52, 53, 57,
       59,
  Martha 33,
  Samuel 48,
INNIS.
  James 10,
  Katherine (Wife of James) 10,
IRELAND.
  Sarah 54,

JACKSON.
  David 24, 79,
  Elizabeth 11,
JACOB.
  Evan (Servt. to Nathaniel Thrift) 75,
JAMES.
  Francis 46, 100.
  Margaret 11,
  Thomas 11,
JEFFEREYS.
  Anne 1, 11,
  Edward 1, 22, 24, 40, 42, (Ord. Keeper, pre-
       sented -47, dismist -87), 61, 62, 65, 73,
       77, 79, 84, 90, 98, 100.
JENKINS
  Thomas 55, 59, 98,
  William 85, 96,
JENNINGS.
  Anne or Margaret (Dau. of John, deced), 48,
       49,
  Henry 40, 41, 43, 67, 68, 85,
  John 48, 50,
  John (deced) 48, 50,
JESPER.
  Thomas 33, 52, 79, 80,

PEARSON.
  James (presented -14), (fined -28), 68, 85,
PEASLEY.
  Redmond 54,
PECK.
  Robert (Levy free -54),
PHELPS.
  Thomas 41,
PHILIPIN.
  Thomas 24,
PHILLIPS.
  Bryan 43, 59,
  George 39, 40, 57, 69, 81, 93,
  James 5, 6, 8, 16, 18, 20, 21, 38, 39, 42, 45.
       56, 57, 59-61, 64, 70, 81, 87, 93,
  James Junr. 7,
  Richard 77,
  William 33, 74,
PILKINTON.
  William 52, 71, 72,
PINCHETT.
  Seaburn 32,
PITTENDRICK.
  Alexander (noncupative Will proved -88),
PITTMAN.
  William 52, 99,
PLEY.
  Elizabeth 61,
POPE.
  Nathaniel 9, 12, 31, 79,
POPE als. BRIDGES.
  Nathaniel (of Westmoreland Co.) 16, 37,
PORT.
  Robert 51,
PORTER.
  James 24,
PORTWOOD.
  Thomas 12,
POTTS.
  Thomas 92,
POUND.
  John 18, 47, 57, 61, 63, 96,
POWELL.
  Edward 32,
  William 18,
PRENTICE.
  Thomas 11,
PRESCOAT / PRESCOTT
  Jane 70,
  Lawrence 40, 41, 70,
PRESSLEY.
  Peter 13, 59, 81,
  Winifred (Wife of Peter, Exrx. of Corbin Griffin,
       deced) 13, 59, 81,
PRICE.
  Joseph 17,

PRIDHAM.
  Christopher 17, 33, 37, 56, 89,
  Mary (Wife of Christopher) 89,
PRITCHETT.
  Christopher 79, 98,
PURVIS.
  George 16,

RADFORD.
  George 22, 39, 42, 58, 60,.63, 69, 77, 99, 100.
  Sarah 96,
RANKIN.
  John (presented -14), 16, (fined -28), 75, 91,
  Penelope (Wife of John, Exrx. of John Overton)
       75, 91,
RATELEPH.
  Robert 54,
REDWOOD.
  Susanna 92,
REEVE.
  Thomas 67,
REYLEY.
  Katherine 77,
REYNOLDS / RENELLS
  Jefferey 78,
  John 3, 10, 19, 24,
  Robert 18, 19, 36,
  Thomas 48,
  William 86,
RICHARDS.
  Lewis 17, 37, 56,
RICHARDSON.
  James 24,
  John (deced) 99,
  Mary (presented -13, 26,), 34,
  Mary (Admrx. of John) 99,
  Roger (presented -14), 29,
  Thomas 16, 40,
  William (presented -14), 29, (fined -36),
RICHENSEN.
  John 1,
RICHISON.
  John 66,
  James 61,
ROARK.
  Edward 54,
ROBERTS.
  John (presented -14), (fined -27),
ROBERTSON.
  William 24,
ROBINSON.
  Christopher 13, 59, 81,
  Frances (Wife of Majr. Wm.) 4,
  Henry 1, 9,
  Judith (Wife of Christopher) 13, 81,
  William 19, 42,   (Robinson, contd.)

SMITH (contd.)
  Eve 17,
  Eve (deced) 37, (Will proved -58), 75, (Inv.
      retd. -88),
  James 12,
  Nicholas 7, (presented -14), (fined -29), 32, 61,
      62, 73, (Justice -74), 77, 83,
  Richard (presented -14), 16, (fined -26),
  Robert 11,
  Thomas 46, 96,
  William 11, 62, 84, 92,
  William (Cordwainer) 6, 21,
  William (on the Hill) 42,
  William (Shoemaker) 42, 63. 64,
  William (Tanner) 52, 66. 69, 71, 72, 85, 98,
      99, 100.
  William (an Admr. of John Howell) 23,
  William Junr. (fined -28),
SMOOT.
  William 3, 12, 15, 33, 45,
SNEAD.
  Charles 98,
SOMMERVILL
  John 58, 72, 87, 98,
  Margaret (Wife of John, Exrx. of Hugh French)
      72, 87, 98,
SPENCE.
  Elizabeth (Wife of Alexander) 99,
  Alexander 92, 95, 99,
SPENDERGRASS.
  James 42,
  James (deced) 74,
  James (Son of James, deced) 74,
  John (Son of James, deced) 74,
SPOO.
  Charles 2,
  Mary 17, 18,
STEELE.
  John Mercht. 63,
  Justin 66, 72, 99,
STEPHENSON.
  William 2,
STEVENSON / STEPHENSON
  James (presented -47), 73, 78, 91,
STEWARD.
  Charles 52, 79, 80,
  Duncan 18,
  Margaret 11,
STIGELEER.
  James 22, 40, 42, 59,
STONE.
  Francis 36, 79, 87, 99,
  Joshua (presented -14), (fined -27), 70, 75,
      86, 96,
  William 7, 21, 24, 50, 79,

STORY.
  James 10, 40, 44. 57, 60, 71, 81, 93,.
  John 42,
  Margaret (Wife of James) 45,
STOTT.
  John 93,
STREET.
  Henry 88,
STROTHER.
  Benjamin 79,
  Dorothy 62,
  James 24, 66,
  Jeremiah 61, 81,
  Robert 79,
  William 54, 79,
SUGGITT.
  Edgcomb 52,
  Elizabeth (an Exr. of John) 65, 74,
  James 12, 16, 19, 21, 37, 48, 52, 56, 58, 67,
      81, 98,
  John (deced, Will proved -9), 25, 34, 65,
  John (an Exr. of John) 65,
  Thomas 52, 74,
SWAMPS.
  Doeg 44, 86, 87,
SWYNEY
  Morgan 22, 23, 41,

TALIAFERRO.
  Richard 10, 41, 61, 69. 70, 80, 85, 94,
TANKERSLEY.
  Richard 55, 72,
TARPLEY.
  James 7, 15,
  John 15, 23, 39, 41, 57, 59, 68,
  John (Father of John Junr.) 59, 81,
  John Capt. (see Justices -1), 10, 16, 19, 25,
      30, 32-34, 36, 37, 46, (apptd. Sherriff
      -49), 53, 77, 79, 80, 86, 98,
  John (Gdn. of John Junr.) 13, 37,
  John Junr. 13, 37, 59, 81,
TAVERNER.
  John 52, 90,
TAYLER.
  Edward 66,
  George Lieut. Colo. (see Justices -1), 24, 37,
      47, 49, 51, 76, 77, 79, 89,
  Joseph 93,
  Richard 7,
  Robert 72,
  Symon 33,
  Symon (Gdn. of John Glow) 9,
  Susanna (Wife of Lt. Colo. George Tayler,
      Widow of Elias Wilson) 77,

WELSH.
  Thomas 76, 91,
  Walter 76,
  Walter (deced) 91,
WESTCOMB.
  James 32,
WHITE.
  Bridget 18,
  Daniel 40, 49,
  George 19, 22,
  John 8, 18, 37, 43, 57, 59, 64, 66. 80, 92,
  Margarett (Wife of John) 18, 37, 43, 44, 57,
      80, 92,
  Richard (presented -14), (fined -26), 76,
  Richard (Son of Mary Northcutt) 3,
  Sarah (Wife of Richard, Widow of Wm. Hanks)
      76,
  Thomas 6-8, 21, 24, 30, 38, 44, 45, 63, 83,
      87,
WHITING.
  Joshua 8,
WILKS.
  William 100.
WILLIAMS.
  David 16, 68,
  Francis 5, 20, 21, 42, 48, 50, 52, 54, 59, 78,
      79,
  John 12, 13,
  Robert 17,
  Thomas 97,
WILLIS.
  John 70, 79,
  John Junr. 52, 58, 67, 86,
  William 52, 62, 70,
WILSON.
  David 40,
  Elias (deced) 77,
  Elias Junr. 77,
  Henry 25, 55,
  James (presented -47, dismist -87), 73, 86,
  John 15, 17, 56, 60, 63.
  Robert 12,
WISDELL.
  Richard 5, 20, 97,
WISE.
  John 54, 61, 81, 99,
WOFFENDALL.
  Adam 24,
  Adam (deced) 5, 20,
  Honor (Exrx. of Adam) 5, 7, 20, 21,
WOOD.
  Elizabeth 93,
  Henry 62,
  Richard 7,
  William (presented -14), 16, (fined -35).

WOODBRIDGE
  William 1, 5, 13, (Bond required -26), 34, 45,
      88, 90,
WOODFORD.
  William 100.
WOODWARD.
  Elizabeth (Admrx. of Wm.) 64, 84,
  Joseph 99,
  William (deced., late of Lancaster Co.) 64,
      84,
WOOLDRIDGE.
  Susanna 92,
WORDEN.
  John 5, 8, 20, 40, 57, 64, 81, 93,
WRIGHT.
  Francis Majr. 55,
  John 25,
  John (Son of Majr. Francis Wright) 55,
  John (Smith) 42,
  Motron (deced) 70, 85,
  Walter 69, 96,
WYNN.
  Thomas 60,

YATES.
  Thomas 16, 41,
  William 46, 58, 60, 66. 67, 71, 72, 85, 99,
  William (Uncle to Wm. Morgan) 3,
YEATMAN.
  John 53,
YOUNG.
  David 20, 38,
  Edward 6,
  John 13,
  Lawrence 60, 81,